Keith Elford has been a consultant to [...] ness, public and voluntary sectors [...] time as a partner in Telos Partners. [...] served as an incumbent and Bish [...] of Guildford. He is currently a minister in secular employment. He is married and has two stepsons. In his spare time, he is an enthusiastic member of two rock bands.

CREATING THE FUTURE OF THE CHURCH

A practical guide to addressing whole-system change

KEITH ELFORD

First published in Great Britain in 2013

Society for Promoting Christian Knowledge
36 Causton Street
London SW1P 4ST
www.spckpublishing.co.uk

Copyright © Keith Elford 2013

All rights reserved. No part of this book may be reproduced or transmitted in any
form or by any means, electronic or mechanical, including photocopying, recording,
or by any information storage and retrieval system, without permission in
writing from the publisher.

SPCK does not necessarily endorse the individual views contained in its publications.

The author and publisher have made every effort to ensure that the external website
and email addresses included in this book are correct and up to date at the time
of going to press. The author and publisher are not responsible for the content,
quality or continuing accessibility of the sites.

British Library Cataloguing-in-Publication Data
A catalogue record for this book is available from the British Library

ISBN 978–0–281–07077–0
eBook ISBN 978–0–281–07078–7

Typeset by Graphicraft Limited, Hong Kong
First printed in Great Britain by Ashford Colour Press
Subsequently digitally printed in Great Britain

eBook by Graphicraft Limited, Hong Kong

Produced on paper from sustainable forests

Contents

Foreword

The Bible is not short of examples of complex organizational processes taking place in the life of the people of God, especially at moments of challenge or threat. Jethro saw that a more dispersed leadership structure was needed for God's people as they waited to enter the promised land. The walls of Jerusalem had to be rebuilt after the years of neglect during the Jewish exile. Deacons were to be appointed if the apostolic ministry of the Church was to be sustained. Decisions had to be made and implemented about the integration of Gentiles into the kingdom of God. Each situation demanded clear leadership, shared vision and cumulative effort. Behind it all, of course, was the providential hand of God guiding and shaping his people. But the God of Israel and Incarnation operates in and through human activity.

What was true then for God's people is true for us today as we hold the providential hand of God and allow that strong and gentle hand to lead us towards the promised land of God's kingdom by steps that require insight and planning, courage and calculation, careful thought and daring determination. As of old, we are called to be clear about who we are, and to live out that calling faithfully in the present conditions of life but always looking to the future that God has for us, moving in that direction with God, hand in hand, step by step.

This short book, written by a person with a great love for God's people and a genuine confidence in God's purposes for his people in the world, takes seriously what we might call *the incarnational principles of God's providence*. With hard-won experience of organizational change, Keith Elford provides some clear and practical advice on how the leadership of the Church in its various spheres, and at its many levels, can rise to the responsibility that we have been given in our age, and become more skilled in our use of the social processes that help us walk in step with the Spirit. The

Church, being and bearing the Body of Christ, is the transformative agent of God's purposes in the world. We can only be so, and do so, if we are a transformed Church. This book, with its practical wisdom, is a valuable tool for that end.

Christopher Cocksworth
Bishop of Coventry

Acknowledgements

I could not have even contemplated this book without the knowledge and learning gained from 12 years of working with colleagues at Telos Partners. I am extremely grateful for that experience, for all my colleagues have taught me and for the direct and invaluable feedback I received about this book at various stages of its development.

The greater part of the learning comes from our clients, of course. My special thanks go to all those I have worked with. I believe that consultancy should operate as a partnership in which the learning goes both ways – I greatly value the trust and friendship that have grown as a result. I would like to thank clients for permission to include examples of their work.

A number of clergy, church officers and bishops provided information, advice and insights during the book's preparation. I have appreciated and valued every conversation, and am particularly grateful for the encouragement and wisdom of the following: Bishop John Gladwin (now retired, he was my boss when I was his chaplain in the 1990s, and a valued friend); Karen West (Archbishops' Adviser on Bishops' Ministry); Julian Hubbard (Director of Ministry for the Church of England); David Jennings (Senior Strategy Officer, Church Commissioners); Malcolm Grundy (the doyen of church writers on leadership and management); and Bishops Christopher Hill, Steven Croft, Tim Thornton and Chris Cocksworth. Many thanks also to David Parry of Christ Church, Barnet and the Revd Trevor Denley of St Aidan's, Fishponds, in Bristol for sharing their stories of growth with me and giving me permission to share them.

I also owe a debt to the clergy and people of St James, Weybridge for offering me a spiritual home and keeping me grounded in the realities of parish life.

My thanks go also to Ruth McCurry and her colleagues at SPCK for giving me this opportunity to get these ideas 'out there'.

Acknowledgements

I greatly appreciate all their help to get the manuscript in the right final shape.

Finally, my wife Annabelle has been a constant source of support and belief during the book's long gestation – to her, a heartfelt 'Thank you'.

Introduction

What is the Church? The question can be answered in familiar theological and poetic phrases: 'The body of Christ', 'The people of God', 'A royal priesthood', 'The new Israel'. But the Church is also a human institution, an organization. In fact it is several such organizations. These all see their core identity in the theological terms above, but they all have an all too human history. Most of them have their origins as organizations in periods and circumstances very far from the communities that first described themselves as the body of Christ.

What happens if we consider the Church as an organization like other organizations? What happens if we apply to the Church what we now know about what makes organizations successful over the long term? These are the simple questions behind this book. The questions and the activity that follows from answering them are not offered as a substitute for prayer, discipleship, spirituality or any of the traditional ways the Church nurtures itself. This book proposes a parallel, not an alternative endeavour, in the conviction that while the Church is more than an organization it is not less than an organization.

Nevertheless, the contention of the book is that applying what we know about organizational development would have a transformational impact on the Church. In the last 20 years in particular there has been a great deal of research and practical learning about what makes organizations sustainably successful. The results of this take us a long way from the managerialism about which many church people are so understandably sceptical. We are not talking about a series of management techniques, still less about management fads. In the 1970s, books were written about improving the administration of the Church by applying the techniques and practices common in private and public-sector organizations.[1] These were, no doubt, full of good practical advice but they were not likely to effect any kind of transformation – their intention was tactical rather than strategic. This book is far more interested in the conditions that enable organizations and those in them to thrive. It is far more about people than mechanics. In fact we will be taken closer to questions of faith than we will to management techniques as commonly understood. In essence it is about taking a more coherent approach to the way we think about and 'do' Church. It is about the benefits that accrue from being more deliberate.

The scepticism with which many people regard management theory is understandable when one contemplates the contents of any bookshop's business section. So much on offer seems shallow and repetitive. 'Management speak' is not attractive and is an easy target for the media and clergy alike. Much of the negativity, however, results from an inaccurate and outdated understanding of what the best people from the business and management worlds are actually saying. This book aims to look a bit deeper.

There is an irony here, of course. A bishop told me about a conversation he had with a businessman from his diocese. The businessman offered the bishop his help in matters where his experience could be useful. The bishop replied that he would be delighted to accept the offer and wondered if he could offer his help in return. The businessman was puzzled – what did the bishop mean? The bishop asked him how long his business had been in existence ('15 years', the businessman replied), and then pointed out that he worked for an organization that had been in business for 2,000 years – perhaps it knew something about what worked?

I have worked as a consultant to organizations of many kinds, including religious bodies, for over 14 years. One of the key principles my colleagues and I employ is that the greatest experts in any business's issues are those who work for it and know it inside out. Nothing this book says is intended to minimize the knowledge and experience of people who belong to the Church, or the learning available from its venerable history.

The Church seems to suffer less from a lack of knowledge, experience or ability than from a lack of confidence and of rigour in applying what it knows. 'The future the Church is currently in' is somewhat grim – if we do not change, I do not see a positive future for it. But rather than wanting to encourage gloom, I believe we can and should act to create a different and better future. The Church has plenty of resources available in its people, history, theology and Scriptures. To some extent this book will be about rediscovering principles and practices that have their origins in the Church – it was, after all, one of the first organizations, as we have come to understand the term, and words like 'values' and 'vision' were religious before they were managerial.

I long to see the Church become confident again in its ability to take control of its own destiny. One of the things a confident institution does is engage positively with ideas and insights that originate outside itself – it is insecure and consequently defensive organizations that reject good news from the world outside.

Despite this, some may be put off by the secular provenance of a great deal of the material in this book. I have noticed that many people in the Church do not want to move until they have developed a special Christian theology of organizations or leadership or whatever the subject may be. Perhaps it will help if I explain my thinking on this. I am wary of the need to put the words 'Christian theology of' in front of everything, as if there is on every subject a special Christian truth accessible only to religious people who understand God to be the Creator of this world and his Spirit to be the source of all life and truth. So there is no 'Christian' truth, as in truth that is the special preserve of the Church or of Christians, but only God's truth, or *the* truth. So I am happy to learn from secular sources. This does not mean I do not view them through a Christian lens or appraise them carefully, but I do not feel the need to go through an exhaustive process before taking action. The theological reflection can be done – and may well be better done – as we work with the concepts in practice.

Much of what I have to say is based on my own work as a parish priest and Bishop's Chaplain as well as, latterly, a coach and organizational consultant. It is intended to offer both an intellectual and practical framework for anyone interested in effecting a sustainable transformation of the Church, whether at national or local level. It is in part a thought piece, aimed at exploring the issues that will arise when we set out on the path to tackling organizational problems, and intended to provoke and stimulate. At the same time it offers a route map, a process, a how-to guide for those who want to take action. A complete programme is presented in the order things are best tackled, but it is not intended to be completely prescriptive – life is rarely, if ever, as neat as such a programme might imply. Experience shows that organizations can do things in the 'wrong' order and not as fully as I might prefer, and still get good results. The process set out here could be characterized as an organized way of holding an honest conversation among concerned parties. The quality of the conversation and the willingness to include all those who need to be included are what matter most.

The book is in two parts. Part one is more philosophical and sets the scene by describing the challenges facing the Church today. Many of these problems and issues are relatively well known but the intention is to demonstrate the need to think more strategically and less tactically. I then describe my approach to organizational renewal, as well as the intellectual framework that informs the rest of the book.

Part two begins by describing the process I recommend, and each subsequent chapter describes a stage in that process. These chapters also have philosophical passages but are more practical, offering a step-by-step how-to guide for those who want to take action. Each chapter begins with a description of the thinking that informs the process: these passages are intended to be a relatively objective account. This is followed by a consideration of questions and issues that will arise in the Church: these sections are intended to help, provoke and stimulate, and more frankly represent my views. Each chapter concludes with a sometimes detailed account of how the process can be implemented: these sections are intended to guide action.

I hope that disagreement with particular observations will not impair the book's overall usefulness. And although it is argumentative, I do not offer answers to the questions raised by the thinking and the process, or put forward my views on the purpose, values or future strategy of the Church. The point of the book is to suggest a framework and a process that will allow readers to find their own answers.

Who is it aimed at? It will be most obviously useful to people holding positions of leadership in the Church – clergy, bishops – but it is intended to be relevant to anyone who wants to influence the future of the Church for good. Because I am an Anglican and know the Church of England best, it is to that Church I explicitly address what follows. Although I believe a national programme is both possible and desirable, the description of the implementation of the process is focused on the diocese and the parish – the two main units of the Church of England. Readers should be able to adapt the process for other Anglican organizations or other Churches relatively easily.

A few years ago I met the Superior General of a Roman Catholic order of Sisters. The Congregation provides care for the aged in five regions across the world. The Sisters are a dedicated, capable, down-to-earth and charming group of Christian women – and very good indeed at providing care. They were facing a number of difficulties, however: they were becoming fewer, ageing and could see a time in the not too distant future when they would be none; their way of working was inefficient and outdated; public expectations and government regulation were ever more demanding and difficult to keep up with; their buildings were, in many cases, no longer fit for purpose, in need of major refurbishment or replacement; the financial future looked bleak. Faced with this, the Sisters' default strategy had been to close houses – about half of them over a 30-year period.

We worked together for four years, following the thinking and the process set out in this book. The Sisters have reversed the policy of closure and are thinking about expansion. The ministry is being run ever more efficiently and the Sisters are seeing significant gains in financial performance, with the promise of further improvement. Buildings are being gradually repaired or renewed. None of this has been at the expense of the core beliefs, values or caring ministry of the Sisters – on the contrary, a renewal of the sense of mission and purpose has been at the heart of the process. Above all, perhaps, for the first time in a generation the Congregation is looking to the future with hope.

Yes, a religious order is a more discrete entity than the Church of England; yes, its commitment to a common ministry provides a focus less readily available in the Church. But do not under-estimate the Sisters' achievement at a time when the active orders, in particular, are in real trouble – they still have plenty to do, but they have come a very long way. The national Church, dioceses or parishes can take similar action with similar results *if they really want to*. It can be done.

Part 1

UNDERSTANDING THE ISSUES

1

Face the facts

The Church is one of the world's most successful organizations yet also extremely vulnerable in the West. The Church of England is deeply embedded in the social fabric, is still a major force in the land and does have its success stories – but it faces many problems and cannot, on the basis of recent and current trends, contemplate the future with a great deal of hope.

This chapter describes the challenges facing the Church and clergy and bishops operating in the current environment. It acknowledges that there has been change, intended to respond to shifts in that environment, and recognizes the potential evidenced in growing churches and dioceses. It sets out the contention that, overall, changes have been too local and piecemeal to constitute an adequate response, and argues that what is required is a more fundamental, strategic, rethink of the Church's role and operation. The chapter begins with some remarks about the Churches more generally before concentrating on the Church of England.

> **Cameo 1: Some of my own recent experiences and impressions of the Church**
>
> Working with the ministry team of a united benefice in Lincolnshire that consists of three groups – a total of 24 churches covering over 100 square miles, served by three full-time clergy and a number of voluntary lay ministers. Not sure whether to regard this as evidence of a dreadful decline or an exciting new model of rural ministry – probably both.
>
> Reading Rowan Williams' remarks about the coalition government pursuing policies that electors did not vote for and thinking that his critique would have more weight if the Church of England did not appear to be so dysfunctional itself.

Looking at the agenda of the July 2011 General Synod and feeling some despair at the endless list of committee reports – but rather encouraged by the devotion of a whole morning to more informal work in small groups.

Sitting in my own parish church on a Sunday morning, hearing fine music and thoughtful preaching, and feeling encouraged by the numbers of people in the congregation.

Talking to a bishop who confidently and energetically described his commitment to working strategically in his diocese. According to him it is both true that the Church is in big trouble and that there is no reason why it cannot survive and thrive by grasping and shaping the future now. But then, he remarked, 'I am something of a lone voice.'

A conversation with a vicar – I said I probably would not return to stipendiary ministry, to which he responded with a rather despairing sigh: 'You don't need the s**t that goes with it, do you?'

Challenges arising from a changing context

The Church is still at the centre of many people's lives. There are many who find it a haven and a blessing in times of great difficulty, and many who cannot imagine life without it. And many like it just as it is! Some of my own recent experiences of the Church are recorded in Cameo 1.

What are yours? And how do you interpret them? Every part of the Church will have its particular concerns, but how would you describe the issues facing your part of the Church? What are the challenges and what are the opportunities? A great deal in the Church is admirable and even exciting, but there seem few reasons to believe it is likely to address its many challenges successfully. The world in which it operates has changed – so has the Church, but has it changed comprehensively enough? I do not think so.

Still a powerful force

The Church's achievements are immense. We know how long it has been around (for a business, even 50 years is an exceptionally long

4

life span), and what organization has done more to shape British life? There is much to admire in the Church now. The Church of England has a presence in every locality in the country it serves. Its churches generate funds of £900m[1] annually and rates of giving are rising. In 2005 there were 3,018,800 people attending Christian churches on Sundays in the UK.[2] The Church of England has 28,000 people in active, licensed ministries.[3] Church organizations provide a vital contribution to the provision of care for those who need it in this country and beyond. Church schools are highly sought after by parents for both their values and their good academic results. The Church is the principal source of a large proportion of the volunteers on whom other third-sector organizations depend. Its leaders still have political influence. At regional and local level the Church still has a valued civic role. For all that the Church does not have the wealth or power it once possessed, it is still a substantial operation. The vast majority of Britons will engage with the Christian Church at some stage in their lives – even if it is only the final stage.

The way many of the Churches are structured is often seen as a weakness because of the problems it creates for control from the centre and for media people anxious to find out what 'The Church' thinks. It is equally possible to argue that the Church provides an example of just the kind of distributed leadership considered so desirable by many management experts. The Church of England, the Methodist Church and many others give enormous discretion and independence to their local representatives and rely to a large extent on their energy and initiative. Although this approach creates many difficulties, it has been, and remains in many ways, highly successful.

Declining attendance and belief

The Church undeniably faces a number of problems, however. Although it is frequently valued and effective at local level it is a fact that attendances have been declining over the last few decades. The numbers are alarming: according to the Christian Research group, half a million people stopped going to church between 1998 and 2005.[4] It is often countered that patterns of churchgoing are changing and that more people are attending monthly rather than weekly, also that there is a shift to churchgoing during the week. This is true, and recent figures suggest that, overall, decline is slowing. But however you measure it, the trend is still relentlessly downward – average weekly attendance in the Church of England declined by over 10 per cent between 2000 and 2010. And if the current trend continues it will get much worse. Anyone who attends church regularly will have noticed that congregations tend to be composed of older people. The majority will be over 50 or even over 60. It is the loyalty of these older people that is keeping the numbers as high as they are, but what will happen when this generation passes? The projections of the church statisticians envisage a calamitous further decline so that by 2040 the Church will have become a rump, in business only because of its considerable historic assets.

Attendance is not the only issue. To what extent does Christianity have a real grasp on the public mind? Newspapers may have a lot to say about the Church's politics, and many people still identify themselves as Christian in surveys. Nevertheless, although the evidence may be anecdotal, many will find it hard to disagree with Monica Furlong that:

> Children who do not come from churchgoing homes – as I did not – now grow up largely ignorant of Christian ideas in a way unimaginable half a century ago . . . The comments about religion by journalists in the press and on television . . . suggest that even the basic Christian ideas are no longer understood by university-educated people, still less by others. Indeed even churchgoers can reveal an ignorance of the main elements of Christian belief.[5]

Nearly all Christian activities are less well supported than they used to be and the Church's beliefs and ideas are less well understood.

Declining finances
Inevitably the decline in attendance has had a negative effect on the Church's finances, especially in the York archdiocese, although increasing rates of giving have softened the impact considerably. How long can the Church rely on increases in rates of giving

to make up for the decline in the number of givers? It seems unlikely that it will be able to maintain the full range of current parochial, diocesan and national ministries. In a number of dioceses, centralized ministries have been reduced to save money. There has been a heartening increase in the number of ordinands in the Church of England but there are fewer full-time, paid ministers – partly because many more offering themselves for professional ministry choose to be 'non-stipendiary' and partly because the Church cannot afford to pay for them. The provision today of adequate pensions for clergy is, of course, absolutely necessary, but it absorbs a great deal of the Church's resources – for dioceses (funding new pensions since 1998) and for the Church Commissioners (paying out on those from the pre-1998 scheme). The Church has an extremely valuable asset base, particularly in property. It should perhaps consider how best to use these assets to generate growth before it finds itself critically short of people and cash.

Inward focus

When all the factors are taken into account, it does not seem unduly alarmist to say that things could become much worse yet – the patient may not survive. In this context it is mystifying to outsiders that the Church has become preoccupied with internal squabbles over matters that are often seen as largely settled in the rest of society – the status of women and of homosexuals. These debates absorb a great deal of energy and are very damaging to the Church's reputation. The internal focus is a classic symptom of lost direction and confidence.

Uncertainty about role: the impact on church leaders

Burdens on the clergy

The difficulties facing the Church create heavy daily burdens and dilemmas for those whose task it is to lead the Church. There is a cost associated with the confusion and uncertainty that exists. Many ministers, especially Church of England parish priests, still find themselves valued and respected members of their local communities, though this is not universally true. The majority of clergy are dedicated, conscientious, imaginative and intelligent and have effective ministries. It can be terribly hard going, however. The minister now operates in a world that has become more complex and more demanding.

One major consequence of the changes in the world served by the Church is that clergy are far less clear on their role. Many see themselves as pastors or priests *as against* leaders of organizations. Yet in practice they find themselves pushed ever more into the latter role. Financial pressures mean that the smaller cadre of stipendiary clergy find themselves with larger responsibilities (such as several churches), have to shoulder a considerable administrative burden and may have less assistance in discharging it. The benefice I worked with in Lincolnshire (see Cameo 1) is an extreme but not entirely untypical example. This is a completely different model of ministry, heavily dependent on lay ministers. Rectors are more like 'mini-bishops' – one diocese is consciously adopting that model.

Much of what clergy do may not be what they believed they were ordained for. They are surrounded – in their congregations – by people who know what *they* want and keep saying it. The majority of people beyond the Church do not know what the minister does. Most are curious, friendly and open-minded when they actually meet the minister, but in a large parish will only connect with the Church infrequently. Clergy are uncertain whether their role is primarily to 'run the Church' or to represent the faith in the wider community – it is increasingly difficult to do both. The Churches may be less influential than they were, though they are probably busier.

One of the inherent challenges of Christian ministry is the difficulty of measuring success. Priestly or pastoral ministry does not lend itself to clear outcomes – it is all much more nebulous. The negative impact of this feature of ministry is greatly intensified today. As a result of role confusion, ministers are working long and stressful hours *and* are often unsure what they are achieving by doing so. Most clergy feel under a pressure to perform, to have an impact, and consequently –

whatever they may say to the contrary! – are anxious about the numbers of people in the pews because it is the default measure of success.

Some ministers I know seem stressed, perhaps depressed, and many are remarkably paranoid about their congregations and about their superiors. It appears, fortunately, that this is not what clergy actually report. A 2011 survey suggests 'a more optimistic picture of the experiences of ministry than many would have previously thought',[6] and relatively high levels of engagement and low levels of burnout compared to people in similar occupations. The clergy life is rewarding if 'exhausting and demanding' in the words of one survey respondent.

The impossible lives of bishops

To get a sense of the life of a bishop you have merely to contact a diocesan bishop's office and try to arrange an appointment. You will be lucky to find a gap in three or four months' time. If you ask what the bishop is doing the answers might include: conducting a deanery visit, sitting on a committee, visiting a local company, on duty in the House of Lords, chairing a national body, officiating at a confirmation, meeting his rural deans, holding a staff meeting, meeting a journalist – and so on. Most bishops are passionate about how they define their role and will speak eloquently about the meaning of episcopacy. In practice most are juggling a range of voracious demands on their time. Most see themselves as ambassadors for the Church in their diocese and so will devote a lot of time to engaging with the wider community – though this typically involves many functions with the great and good it will also involve attempts to engage with the lives of ordinary people through visits and supporting local community projects. Bishops also soon acquire national responsibilities – chairing church bodies or religious charities or taking a seat in the House of Lords. A diocese has a significant structure of its own and a bishop will soon find diocesan synod, board of finance and bishop's council taking up time and attention. And as there is the natural desire of parishes to receive a visit from their pastor-in-chief, a programme of visits is rapidly organized. And as bishops take their responsibility to their clergy seriously too (whatever many may think), there will be any number of one-to-one meetings. The bishop also has a critical liturgical role, reflected in the round of confirmations and ordinations.

This is an immense job. A diocese is an organization with a budget of several million pounds and a workforce of many hundreds, and leading it is a considerable challenge, especially when one considers how little direct authority a bishop really has. Most dioceses face financial difficulties and the constant pressure to do more with less.

Bishops also have the unenviable task of acting as a focus of unity in an increasingly factional Church. They may well find that many of their churches barely recognize their ministry as a result of theological or ecclesiological disagreement. They are constantly asked to comment on matters of media concern (for example, the latest controversial episcopal appointments in The Episcopal Church in the United States of America), and know that to say anything remotely interesting will only result in a flood of abusive letters – and they *are* abusive – from the diocese and beyond, and at the same time make life more difficult for other bishops who will be asked to comment on what the first bishop said. Bishops quickly become reluctant to rock the boat.

Of course it is true that bishops have resources not available to other clergy. They have support staff, a chaplain, suffragan bishops, archdeacons and so forth. But these teams are not always well used. The culture of employment in the Church of England means that bishops are stuck with the staff they inherit for far longer than CEOs in corporations – I know one bishop who finally assembled a team he had appointed himself after being in post for 11 years. This is a far cry from Jack Welch's advice to those appointed to senior roles to give members of their team lacking the right attitude 'thirty days to shape up or leave'.

What is the role of bishops today? Once again there is not a clear answer, and bishops interpret their roles in highly individual ways. In my experience, the role of organizational leader is frequently the one they are least enthusiastic about.

Years of change

Of course, over the last 50 years the Church has not stood still and has made many innovations. The following are some examples:

- The Church's worship is different: there is new, more contemporary language and more options and flexibility in its liturgy; there has been a revival of church music in contemporary style (chiefly, though not exclusively, under the influence of the new Pentecostalism); churches offer 'family' services aimed at parents and young children.
- Many church buildings have been re-ordered to make them more inclusive for worship and more useful to the wider community. These and other developments have made the Church more accessible to many.
- The Church's ministry is no longer a male, clerical preserve and is more widely shared. Most denominations now have women ministers even if women are less likely to be found in the most senior roles.
- More church members recognize that they too have ministries within or beyond the church community.
- Recognizing that people know little about Christianity but remain interested in faith, many churches have developed courses for enquirers. Some have developed their own style, others have used templates, of which the Alpha course is the most well known.

There have been a number of national programmes, some of them ecumenical, not all official. Indeed, the ecumenical movement is one of them. The 1990s was designated a 'Decade of Evangelism', though without conspicuous success. The Church of England currently sponsors Fresh Expressions, a movement designed to develop and encourage new ways of 'being church' – ways more attuned to modern society. These might include meeting in different places, such as a school, or in different ways, such as online. We have also been urged to create 'mission-shaped' churches. The Alpha course, again, is a good example of a national movement with unofficial origins.

The fact is, however, that the Church has not succeeded in halting or reversing the downward trend in attendance of the last 50 years.

The national Church in today's world

A failure to adapt to the new context

My contention is that the Church's particular problems stem from one larger problem. The Churches are still struggling to come to grips with what it means to be part of a secular, multicultural society, to adapt to the huge transformations in its environment. British Christianity has largely operated in a context of state sponsorship and cultural dominance. The Church became used to power, and even the dissenting churches operated in an environment where they were defined against that background. These conditions no longer exist (even though the Church of England remains established), and the Church has not yet fully adapted to the new reality.

In the past the Church of England, in particular, occupied an unassailable position in English society. It may be that the numbers of those truly committed to its beliefs were always smaller than it might have appeared from attendance records, but the Anglican clergyman of the seventeenth, eighteenth and nineteenth centuries operated against a background of deference, shared worldviews and assumptions and a common vocabulary. Of course the picture has never been as neat as that, and much has always been contested, but in general the Church was an accepted and central part of a relatively homogenous culture in which it enjoyed considerable moral, social and political influence. Today the context is utterly different. Society is democratic, egalitarian, composed of multiple faiths and cultures and increasingly secular. When has the Church consciously addressed this in the round? The context has changed utterly but the mental and 'operating' models have not – or at least not sufficiently.

Some suggest there may be as many 'true believers' as ever. According to this argument, Christianity never had the grip on the soul of the Church's members that churchgoing numbers might have suggested. Those who no longer feel obliged to attend have simply stopped going. At the same time we have stopped being 'joiners' and English society is now characterized by 'believing without belonging'. Has the Church really understood this and responded to it?

Addressing the big issue

The initiatives of recent years have clearly had some impact but they have not so far addressed the big issue: the challenge of being the Church, of being Christian, in modern society. The Church of England faces an even more specific version of this general question, namely (as one bishop put it to me), what does it mean to be the national Church in a secular country? This cannot be fixed by initiatives of the kind described earlier, which are too piecemeal, too isolated and not connected to or by a coherent understanding of what the Church is for and where it is going. This is the critical challenge – the Church must articulate what it means to be the Church in a society like ours. It must articulate where it is going in a society likely to develop as ours is. We need an overarching framework that will give particular actions meaning and real traction.

The Church's finances, for example, will not be repaired by cost-cutting or by fundraising projects – getting the money right is a consequence of getting other things right. If the Church is able to articulate its purpose and direction in a compelling way, it will attract adherents who will give to enable the vision they share to be realized.

Ideally there would be a recognition from the centre of the need to create this framework for the Church of England as a whole – and energy put into making it happen. At the moment there is little sign of this. It is hardly surprising, then, that the pattern of isolated initiatives and piecemeal changes tends to be replicated at diocesan and parish level. The dioceses and parishes would have an easier job if they were able to engage with the questions in the context of a national enquiry. In the absence of such a context, however, it is still possible – and necessary – for dioceses and parishes to develop their own framework. And, of course, there are already particular churches and dioceses that have understood this and acted to do it.

Implications for leadership

If the Church is to address these questions it will need leadership both willing and able to think and act strategically. This will involve, for some, a shift in the way they see their role. Many clergy do not understand their role in these terms, nor have they received training to equip them for it – though the situation is improving. Bishops may well feel poorly prepared for their task – they are unlikely to have led an organization of anything like the complexity and scale before. There is little or nothing by way of formal training that might go some way to making up for the lack of experience.

One of the reasons the Church of England needs to develop a strategic rather than merely tactical response to its challenges is that it would improve the lives of its leaders immeasurably. As I have suggested, both bishops and parish clergy play multiple and sometimes confused roles, are overworked and often lack a framework that gives focus to activity and allows meaningful assessment of progress. This combination adds to stress and contributes to illness and depression. Many priests find the old model of the omnicompetent independent priest oppressive as it tends to penalize weaknesses rather than reward strengths. Clergy aspire to teamworking but find it hard to achieve.

If the Church at its various levels had a clearer picture of what it is doing and how it intends to act, it would be much easier to clarify the role of its leaders. This would not be a matter of creating a new template and forcing everyone into it. It should be possible to agree some common features of leadership roles, but the main thrust of the change would be to enable bishops and priests to describe and then make their particular contributions to a larger vision. If a strategy exists it becomes possible to allow individuals to play to their strengths in complementary ways. Teamworking becomes a real possibility and clergy can experience greater support and affirmation of their strengths instead of a sense of failure about the things they are less good at.

Signs of hope

One of the more interesting features of the current position is that there are plenty of examples of the Church bucking all the trends. There are many places where the Church of England is doing new things and where it is growing.

Take the parish of Christ Church, Barnet, for example. In September 2012, at six o'clock on a Friday evening, 100 members of Christ Church set out from the church to walk to all the schools in the area with which they had connections. The walk lasted 24 hours and 60 miles. The oldest participant was 98 years old, the youngest a member of a group of Brownies. The event raised £13,000 towards the Open Door Appeal, a project to set up a new facility for old people in Barnet in the building next door to the church.

This building had once belonged to the church, had been the church school, but was later sold to the Red Cross. In 2003 a Trust was set up for the purpose of buying it back. In the meantime Christ Church had developed its work with older people, which includes a weekly fellowship meeting and an annual holiday club that sees the church hall transformed into a range of exotic destinations. The trustees realized that the 'elderly' are actually a diverse group of people ranging from age 60 to 90 plus – they could only be properly catered for through a much wider set of activities and opportunities than the church hall allowed. The church raised £330,000 and bought the building, and is currently working hard – and professionally – to raise a further million for the required internal transformation.

Or consider the parish of St Aidan, Fishponds, in Bristol. The Revd Trevor Denley retired a few years ago from a career in engineering and was ordained as a part-time, non-stipendiary priest in charge of St Aidan's, a church with a small congregation of around 30. Trevor came with a perspective learnt from the business world: you have always to be prepared to change or die. He also believed that even good products need marketing. He had been an active member of St Aidan's for many years but believed the 'church at the top of the hill' had managed to make itself invisible. He led his team in praying for vision. The result was a resolution to become the 'eyes, ears, hands and feet of Christ in our area'. The strategy designed to deliver this vision was a simple one: get out there. The church holds concerts and participates in the community fair, and Trevor is involved in all the schools, frequently invited to contribute on moral issues. With no full-time priests, lay people have accepted responsibility for specific ministries such as youth and pastoral care. The determination to look outward was reflected in the decision to ensure that the church paid its parish share every year *and* gave money away to good causes on top – something not achieved in many years. In the first year the church gave away £1,000; this year it was £2,500. Trevor is most concerned to ensure that the church is a positive influence in the community – this matters more to him than numbers in church. Nevertheless, 'Messy Church' was introduced and is attended every Wednesday by up to 20 infants and children with no previous connection to the church.

We are used to hearing about stories of innovation and growth involving churches in the Evangelical tradition like Christ Church, Barnet. But it's not only the Evangelicals – as the story of St Aidan's illustrates, there are examples of healthy, growing Churches across traditions of churchmanship.

And there are dioceses where the overall trend is growth in attendance: the dioceses of Southwark, Hereford, Newcastle, London and Canterbury all had more people going to church in 2010 than in 2000.[7] Southwark showed a remarkable increase of 7.57 per cent. Impressive growth has happened where there have been innovations specifically designed to reach new audiences. The Fresh Expressions movement has brought 30,000 people – not counted in any other church attendance surveys – to a new form of Church. On average, parishes with Fresh Expressions of Church aimed at children have 15 new children on Sundays or 25 during the week; those with Fresh Expressions aimed at adults have 25 more adults on Sunday or 20 during the week; parishes with Fresh Expressions total 40 more people attending every week. The growth is not only in numbers but in community impact, as the stories of Christ Church and St Aidan's illustrate.

This is not the place to speculate about what has driven growth in the many places we see it.[8] Often the cause is not known or agreed, though the Holy Spirit presumably has something to do with it. From a human point of view some successes may owe more to luck than judgement. Some may be the result of inspired but impermanent leadership and may not be sustainable. Some may be the result of determined and organized programmes, notably Fresh Expressions. In many cases the initiatives of national church bodies may have played a vital role. Whatever the explanation, the point is simple: it shows it can be done. The Church has the potential, and the examples of growth are a powerful riposte to those who believe that secular society is simply too hostile to organized Christian faith to make recovery possible.

Sadly, these stories do not describe the norm. But what if it was like this everywhere? What if we knew how to identify and release potential in a more organized and systematic way? What if we relied less on chance or inspired individuals and created something sustainable? What if we *organized* ourselves to release potential at the national, diocesan and local levels? Can we imagine a Church where the five marks of mission were all evident and alive at every level?

> To proclaim the good news of the kingdom;
> To teach, baptize and nurture new believers;
> To respond to human need by loving service;
> To seek to transform unjust structures of society;
> To strive to safeguard the integrity of creation and sustain and renew the life of the earth.

The environment is difficult, more challenging than optimists tend to allow, but I believe it can be done. The Church of England could act strategically to realize far more of its potential. It could organize itself to flourish by taking deliberate action. This is not about church growth in any narrow sense, but something far more ambitious: an integrated, strategic approach to the renewal of the Church and its mission in all its dimensions. It can be done by *applying an understanding of the factors that influence organizational viability and success.*

The aim of this book is to help leaders at all levels of the Church to understand and then apply these principles through a demanding but essentially simple and effective process. At its heart is the recognition that we can only make the changes that are needed for the Church to be relevant and effective in the future on the basis of a deep understanding of our fundamental identity and vocation. To repeat: this is not offered as an alternative to prayer and faith or to the work of the Spirit, but in the expectation that all these factors will and must work together. It does assume, however, that God requires us to use all the resources and skills available to us rather than 'faithfully' do nothing.

Summary

The Church is one of the most successful enterprises in human history and remains remarkably important today and rich in potential. It is true that it faces grave threats *and* that it could and should be more confident. It can and should look the issues in the eye and address them far more deliberately.

My contention is that the Church will not solve its problems through isolated initiatives and needs to take a more strategic view of what it exists for and how that should be expressed to address the world as it is today – and will be in the future as far as we can judge. But it has little experience of thinking and working strategically; its ministers – with significant exceptions – do not see themselves as strategic leaders; and many of its most senior leaders lack the necessary skills and experience – a point recognized by the recent launch of leadership development programme for bishops. Ultimately the Church of England needs a national solution, but that should not stop anyone in the Church from addressing the questions to the extent possible at their level. This will, of course, be a project that reflects and takes into consideration both the larger trends I have described and particular local issues. This book is intended to help those who want to take up the challenge.

2

Get organized

People who are serious about achieving something *organize* themselves to do it. They do not rely on chance or serendipity. I am going to discuss the 'principles of organizational success' and 'the key functions of the viable organization'. That may not sound exciting, but it leads to the conclusion that the Church, like any organization, must be ready at any moment to abandon everything, except its soul and its vocation, and enter a new world – this being both a key principle of organizational success and a theological imperative. If we cannot do this, we will not survive.

To talk about organizational success is certainly not to advocate the adoption of managerial techniques or more elaborate processes in the name of 'good practice'. On the contrary, there has been too much of that already and the result has been to increase the Church's tendency to bureaucracy, making it less nimble, more inward looking and less able to act in response to the way the world is changing.

No, this is about something more fundamental, exciting and spiritual, namely the 'whole system' – a comprehensive renewal of the Church that takes more account of our understanding of our mission and our soul.

Cameo 2: Where do you focus your energies?

An Anglican mission agency was struggling to turn its aspirations for the future into reality. Some in the organization believed that this reflected poorly on the capability of the leadership team and, in particular, on their ability to plan and deliver new projects. As part of a piece of work designed to help the team become more effective, we invited members to track their activity for a week. They recorded what they did, and for how long, each day. At the event, we organized the activity under the three headings explored further in this chapter: managing the present (dealing with the current and day-to-day); creating the future (addressing matters of more long-term, strategic significance); nurturing identity (actively strengthening organizational purpose and values). Here's how the week broke down for the team as a whole:

- Managing the present   55 per cent;
- Nurturing identity   20 per cent;
- Creating the future   25 per cent.

We asked them to suggest how they would prefer it to be:

- Managing the present   37 per cent;
- Nurturing identity   26 per cent;
- Creating the future   37 per cent.

There is no simple right or wrong answer to this question (and degree of energy or focus is more significant than time per se), but the exercise helped the team to see that – in their view – they were simply not giving sufficient priority to the activity designed to realize the vision of the future, or to the articulation of the organization's identity that allows change to be made in a way that commanded support. This is frequently the case.

Organizing our lives

There are certain things we all do to be viable or sustainable or successful – to live the lives we want to live or feel called to live. We all have to manage the day-to-day reality of keeping our personal 'shows on the road'. We make choices about the future on the basis of what we believe is possible or what is necessary to achieve a goal or hang on to what we've got – and on the basis of what we believe is right or valuable or, perhaps, the will of God. Once we have made choices we chart a path to the future and change what we do in the present in order to get there.

We are adept at holding together the different factors at work in making our choices, though the choices themselves may not be easy. There are often tensions. Perhaps we feel called to minister in a deprived area but are concerned about the effect that choice might have on our family. Nor is the execution always easy – it requires some discipline and is usually only doable if the goal is sufficiently important to us. Practising scales on the guitar is not in itself particularly exciting, but playing it in a band certainly is and that is the prize that keeps me working on that particular discipline. Like St Paul, we train in order to win the race.

Of course, many of us become so involved in the day to day that we forget about the future. We usually come to regret that. Things sometimes work out well by accident but usually we experience good outcomes because at some point we have made choices designed to make good things happen. Success is usually in some sense deliberate.

The Trialogue

Here I am going to introduce the model that underpins everything that follows in this book and best describes what effective organizations need to do. It does not come from the business world but was developed by a management scientist named Stafford Beer, who was a leading figure in the science of describing organizations as complex systems, and a remarkable, visionary man. St Paul likens the Church to a body with Christ as the head. Stafford Beer began by examining how fundamental organizational systems such as the human body adapt to their environment and maintain themselves successfully. His thinking is based on an enquiry into what organizations *of all kinds* do to remain viable, and identifies key shared functions and characteristics. He believed that in certain vital respects a department store, a government department, a church or a country or an individual all have similar needs. All organizations are systems and must be seen as a whole if they are to thrive over time. His Viable Systems Model, having been further developed by colleagues of mine,[1] asserts that there are three functions that organizations must attend to in order to be effective and sustainable (see Figure 2.1, overleaf).

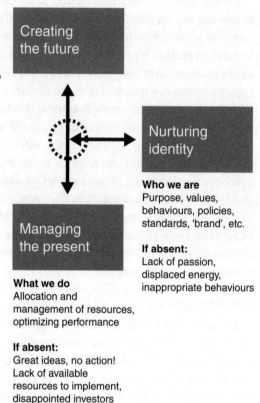

Where we are going
Vision, strategy,
renewal and succession

If absent:
Short-termism, unlikely to
achieve full potential,
lack of direction

Creating
the future

Nurturing
identity

Who we are
Purpose, values,
behaviours, policies,
standards, 'brand', etc.

Managing
the present

If absent:
Lack of passion,
displaced energy,
inappropriate behaviours

What we do
Allocation and
management of resources,
optimizing performance

If absent:
Great ideas, no action!
Lack of available
resources to implement,
disappointed investors

Figure 2.1 Trialogue

Copyright © Peter Dudley, after Stafford Beer. See P. Dudley, 'Quality Management or Management Quality?' PhD dissertation, University of Hull, 2000

In the first place, the viable organization is able to *manage the present*. This is about what we do every day and seeing our activity bear fruit. For a local church it will include the weekly services, the routine administration, regular pastoral visiting and so forth. This is vital: we can only live in the present, and it is here we experience God and the work of God in people's lives. It is right to give attention to improving the way we do our everyday work and to enjoy the good things happening around us. The risk is that managing the present absorbs all our energy and we lose sight of where it is all going and what it is all for.

So the viable organization also acts to *create the future*. It is able to answer the question, 'What will we need to do tomorrow?' In order to create the future we have to stand back and scan the horizon. What is happening in the world? What will we need to do to be relevant in the new world – to ensure that our activity meets tomorrow's needs and not just today's? The organization that does not find time to do this will find that it has become yesterday's news without noticing. It will die.

Third, the adaptive organization is able to *nurture identity*. It is able to answer the question, 'Who are we?' It actively nurtures a shared understanding of identity. How are we to make choices about something as uncertain as the future? Clearly we need good information and a compelling rationale. We will have to make pragmatic judgements about what is possible and achievable. But this will not be enough. If I am making choices for myself I want to do things that matter to me, that are consistent with who I am. Likewise the Church must make choices for the future that are consistent with its identity. If it does not it might survive – but it will not be the Church. Actually it probably won't survive because it will lose the confidence and loyalty of its people. If people think that changes are inconsistent with the organization's identity they will resist them.

These three activities are not separate – they interact and influence one another, like a continuing conversation – hence the term 'Trialogue' to describe it. Leaders need to manage this conversation – this is why good leadership is also an important factor in making organizations viable. The Trialogue is a 'recursive' concept; that is, the questions it poses need to be asked at each level of the organization and, ultimately, by the individual. This means that every layer and group in an organization, every individual, has to make sense of things in these terms. This is why it is so important to involve the organization, its groups and people in shaping any major change.

The Trialogue also sums up and reconciles the claims of the most influential writers on sustainable success in business. Many of these writers emphasize the importance of 'softer' or largely internal factors. The 'Tomorrow's Company Inquiry',[2] for example, concluded that the best businesses understood that organizations are composed of relationships and not just business transactions. People have an emotional investment in organizations, and this includes FTSE 250 companies. High performing businesses recognize this and remain true to corporate purpose and values – the most significant factor in securing and retaining loyalty and commitment, especially from employees. The best companies also have a clear understanding of what constitutes success for all stakeholders – customers, employees, shareholders and the wider community – over the long term. This will include profit and 'shareholder value', but will be much more.

Jim Collins and Jerry Porras argued that the most long-lasting and financially successful companies in the world – outperforming the stock market by a factor of up to 15 times – are united by a determined adherence to a purpose and a set of values that guide all their major decisions.[3] The most effective organizations have the strongest cultures. Jim Collins analysed what had enabled a number of successful major companies to become 'great' and highlighted a number of additional factors.[4] Great companies start by getting 'the right people on the bus' – the right people are not so much those with the greatest skills but with the best attitudes and commitment to leading the organization to greatness. These people face the 'brutal reality' about the business's performance and areas of weakness. They develop a clear understanding of the company 'hedgehog' – the core ideas and competences that drive the business and that must not be compromised. The hedgehog is based on answers to the following questions: 'What are we passionate about? What can we be best in the world at? What drives our economic engine?' These companies are led typically by fiercely determined yet personally humble 'level 5' leaders. Collins concludes that the company that follows these principles will be successful – long-term success is a matter of choice and discipline.

Others see business success in harder or largely external terms. Michael Porter, for example, emphasizes the importance of developing an effective competitive strategy.[5] In other words, successful businesses are good at making choices about how to approach their market as it changes. They make these choices on the basis of a disciplined assessment of the threats and opportunities existing in the market place. And having made the choice, successful companies are then able to execute their strategy efficiently. This focus on execution brings to the fore the hard disciplines of operational management and its accompanying systems and processes.

There is no magic bullet, no method that guarantees success. All organizations are vulnerable to external changes they cannot control. A business may, for good reasons, choose to sell products that it turns out nobody wants. The Church might find there is a declining demand for organized religion that cannot be reversed by anything it does. But organizations can make it far more likely that they will survive and thrive by addressing both hard and soft, internal and external factors in concert, recognizing the importance of a strong culture, making good strategic choices and executing plans well. Success may not be certain whatever they do, but it is rarely, if ever, accidental either, especially over time.

The Church through the lens of the Trialogue

So how does the Church look when considered in this way? The Church, by and large, gives most of its energy to managing the present and often does it well. Many people experience the Church's ministry as positive and valuable, particularly its pastoral care. But this does not alter the fact that it has many problems and does not always manage its affairs well. It is, to put it in commercial terms, losing both customers and money.

The Church gives little time to creating the future. There is little effort focused on understanding its environment and adapting to ensure its continuing relevance. Its attempts to address this issue appear to be confined to isolated initiatives, though there are some encouraging signs that people in the national church institutions are working to achieve a more joined-up approach.

Finally the Church is passionate about its identity but argues about it constantly. It has become a source of disagreement and tension, manifest, for example, in debates about gay clergy and women bishops. These debates are so vehement and sometimes bitter *because* they represent different interpretations of the organization's identity.

The Church cannot be more effective without addressing its life in these three dimensions; without looking at its whole system. If it does not:

- Its continued viability will be threatened.
- It will be slow to innovate and slow to meet the real needs of a changing world.
- It will find itself giving answers to outmoded questions.
- It will not deal with the world as it is but become stuck in the past.
- Its initiatives will lack traction and impact.

This, in fact, is where we are right now.

When the Occupy protestors turned up with their tents on the doorstep of St Paul's Cathedral in protest against the behaviour of the financial institutions, an inconvenience quickly became a public-relations disaster – one that resulted in the resignation of two cathedral clergy including the Dean. The cathedral's reaction seemed confused, contradictory and more concerned with the preservation of its programme of activities than its role as the voice of Christ in the City. The decision to close the cathedral on health-and-safety grounds seemed a huge over-reaction to a few tents. A number of observers asked, 'What would Jesus do?' in a situation like this, and most felt the answer was, 'Not this!'.

I neither know what went on behind the scenes at St Paul's nor want to make assumptions, but it certainly looks as if the Chapter was caught out by an event that did not fit into its normal frame of reference. Anyone can be surprised by the unexpected and the genuinely unpredictable, but there are things the effective organization does to make it less likely to happen and easier to cope with when it does. First, it deliberately and frequently opens its eyes to what is going on beyond its day-to-day world. In this case, it looks beyond its well-established way of working with City institutions and sees that there is a river of discontent growing to which it might need or be in a position to respond. Second, it nurtures and articulates its core purpose and values so that it is unlikely to confuse the core (speaking truth to financial power?) with those things it has got used to doing regularly (putting on the Lord Mayor's Show, for example?). Members of the leadership team spend time thrashing through what these values mean for them individually and as a group, and develop a way of working together that prepares the team for dealing with the unexpected according to clearly identified common principles. That framework appears to have been absent in this case. This is not the same thing as having a media strategy, though that might be part of it: it is really about knowing what you stand for in a way that enables an appropriate and authentic response to new events. Finally, the leadership team knows how to translate these concerns into efficient management of the day to day. It manages. It does not abdicate decision-making to health-and-safety advisers, or sacrifice fundamentals to concerns raised by lawyers.

Or take the recent debacle at General Synod when a small number of laity frustrated the clear will of the vast majority of Anglicans to allow women to become bishops. The failure of the vote revealed a deeply disappointing lack of vision, leadership and management. The debate itself was meant to be about the implementation of a principle already agreed. In the event the contributions were courteous and generous but simply rehashed all the old arguments. The party lines were rarely transcended. Nothing could have better illustrated the extent to which the Church is a prisoner of tired and entrenched positions about its identity. The debate cried out for a new perspective, for a fresh vision of what the Church of England is, should or could be – but none was forthcoming. We desperately need new ground to stand on. The failure of senior leaders in the Church to provide some hint at least of what that new and better territory might look like represents a serious failure of leadership. And on top of all this, losing the vote at the climax of a 20-year process is a colossal failure of basic management.

But the Church of England is unique . . .

Of course, the Church of England has characteristics that distinguish it from other organizations. This leads a number of people to believe that the Church cannot be treated in the way one might approach other organizations, either because it is not 'appropriate' or because it is too difficult. Neither of these objections is acceptable (there is far too much special pleading in the Church), but renewing it does present some particular features and challenges.

The Church is not a business

The Church is not like Tesco – it is neither a business nor a single organization. The Church of England is 43 dioceses, each independent, each with a large number of parishes led by independent officers – the clergy. There is limited capacity to drive change or create a corporate view of the world. This is true structurally – and perhaps even more so culturally.

The aim is not to turn the Church into a corporate machine. There is no need to try to change it into something it is not – in fact that would be a great mistake and counterproductive. It would, in any case, hardly be possible. Protecting and sustaining the essential identity of the organization is at the heart of the approach. The aim is, however, to create a more coherent, purposeful and relevant approach to the challenges facing the Church today and in the future.

There is a tendency in the 'third sector' to harbour unrealistic notions about large companies. It is true that leaders in those organizations possess formal executive powers not usually available in the Church and exercise them within a more straightforward management structure. All this makes it easier to 'get things done', but it would be a fantasy to imagine that the chief executive or anyone else has control over an organization of many hundreds or thousands of people. All organizations depend ultimately on consent and engagement rather than the exercise of power – the capacity of individuals and groups to resist change is great. Any organization will only be able to mobilize people if those people have helped to create the future; if they 'own' it. The failure to understand this point lies behind many corporate failures.

We do not know if the Church of England as a whole can or cannot unite around a common vision or strategy, because it has never been tried, or not since its first 50 or 60 years. It would not be simple, because the 'centre' has little direct authority over the dioceses, nor the dioceses over their parishes. In addition, it is not easy to get the centre – Lambeth, Commissioners, House of Bishops and all the other national church bodies – on the same page. But with sufficient determination and resolve it could be done, through a process of influence and engagement.

The Archbishops would have to lead it – they could if they chose to. It could be done while respecting and preserving the Church's very considerable diversity. But while we wait, perhaps in vain, for that day, there is certainly no reason why a diocese or a deanery or a parish or a Sunday School teaching team should not act to create its future.

Which Church of England are we talking about?

The Church of England exists in several different modes. It is – and this list is by no means exhaustive – a national political institution; a large number of local congregations; several Christian traditions; a religious resource for non-members; and a vital part of the landscape. How can any process take account of all these modes?

Another way of putting this is to think of the Church of England as an organization with a large number of stakeholders, all of whom have to be considered in any proposal to change it. Many other organizations have similar – if less complex – challenges. Marks and Spencer, for example, is not just a retailer of clothes and food. It is a repository and guardian of British middle-class values and mores; has a place in national life; is a major employer; and is part of the landscape. M&S has to consider all these factors if it wishes to modernize itself – we can debate how successful it has been ('Your M&S') but it never occurs to anyone that it cannot be done.

All this means is that the discussion about identity and stake-holder needs in the Church is more complex – not that it is impossible.

The Church of England has a much longer time-horizon than a company

If you place a frog suddenly in hot water it will leap out imme-diately. If you heat the water gradually with the frog already in it, it will sit there until the water boils and kills it.

Some people seem to believe that the Church does not need to put energy into considering how tomorrow will require something different from today. Perhaps this is because the environment for religion changes so slowly that people do not notice the change, or imagine that there is plenty of time to adapt without making a particular effort. But this is a dangerous error, especially now.

Businesses, of course, exist in a fast-moving environment: they know this even if they sometimes forget. Global brands are built on the skilful exploitation of a particular set of market conditions that can alter quickly. Microsoft, for example, became the largest company in the world on the basis of a massively expanding mar-ket for PCs and the software to drive them. In the last five years or so, it has faced competition from new companies and new technologies – such as Google and 'cloud computing' and the shift from PCs to integrated digital platforms – at a time when its traditional market has become saturated. Companies can and do rise and fall in short periods because the business environment changes rapidly.

The 'religious environment' changes over much longer periods. The Church of England did not have to develop its capacity to 'create the future' in the past because it operated in a relatively stable and secure 'market'. That market is now changing and ever more swiftly – it has been doing so for 50 years at least. We are in a new world and we do not have the skills to respond to it – we have not needed them in the past, or not to this degree. It is not that the Church cannot or does not change – it can and has. But now the need to adapt exceeds its capacity to respond. Incremental change will not be enough.

If the Church is not able to adapt its 'products and services' to meet the changing needs of its market, it will not survive except perhaps in a much reduced form. This is not to say that it must simply adapt its message to meet modern tastes. The challenge is more subtle: it is to present itself to the world in a way both relevant to its audience *and* true to its identity.

Church as God's Creation

Some may think the current difficulties are only one episode in a long story. The Church has survived plenty of challenges in the past and will do so again. People will always need the message of the gospel; God will not desert his Church; the Church has demonstrated its longevity and resilience over many years. The keys of heaven and hell have been given to the Church, and the gates of hell shall not prevail against it. But we cannot afford to think this way. The gospel may be eternal, the universal Church may be eternal, but the Church of England probably is not. We are in a new situation and it is far from clear that it will turn out as we would like without positive action.

Do we really want to change?

But here is the really big issue, the very elephant in the room: How much does the Church really want to face its challenges and change to meet them? How much do *you* want to change? For many of its ordinary members the Church works very well as it is. It is a familiar, comforting world to hide away in and though there's nothing wrong with hiding some of the time, you cannot make it a way of life. Never mind that most of the time 95 per cent of the population have little or nothing to do with the Church. How many church members are galvanized by a vision of transformed communities – of a Church that truly exists for those who are not its members?

Are the clergy themselves tempted by nostalgia? A bishop told me that he has to deal with newly ordained clergy who he describes as 'young fogeys' – men and women who hanker after the past, after the traditional practice of ministry, and want to go back to it, to a world that is simply gone. Many clergy are unhappy about the way things are, but change is even more threatening. Insecurity and lack of confidence do not create enthusiasm for the new and unknown. To change might mean acknowledging the huge gap between the Church's rhetoric and its reality – we might, for example, have to face the gulf between what it is formally committed to and what even many of its most conservative adherents actually believe.

The Church needs to re-imagine itself, to work out what it means to be the national Church in this modern multicultural post-Christian society. How is it to be heard, taken seriously, make an impact? The old vision of it as a seat of power expired a long time ago. As a senior clergyman with a role at the heart of the establishment said to me recently: 'It's over'. Of course, this is to state the obvious; at one level most people acknowledge it. Yet many still talk and behave as if they did not – as if the Church has some right to demand attention and support; as if it will always be there. The default strategy could be described as 'Keep calm and carry on'. There is a marked reluctance to acknowledge what is happening (to speak of it is regarded as rather negative; letting the side down), let alone address it coherently. The new focus on mission is welcome but will that be enough on its own? Is the Church prepared to create a new future?

To make this possible the Church will need to draw on a deeper and renewed understanding of its purpose and beliefs. It may need to rediscover ideas that have been important at earlier phases in its history and are somewhat neglected today. It might need to remember, for example, that Christianity is future-orientated, teleological, purposeful, forward-moving, going somewhere. The ascendancy of the established Church and the notion of 'a Christian society' perhaps encouraged a rather static view of the religious life. This is not how Christianity started, nor what we believe, formally speaking. Change is built into the Christian understanding of the world – God is always doing 'a new thing'. Our job is to keep our eyes open and embrace it, not to hang on to what has worked well in the past. We are exhorted to leave our old lives and follow Jesus, a leader of no fixed abode, and need to learn to travel a little lighter and expect to do new things as God leads us into tomorrow's new world. It is not easy, of course, and few of us like it.

Most people and most organizations resist change. David Gleicher tells us that dissatisfaction with the present, a vision of a better alternative and clear first steps need to be all in place and in combination be greater than the resistance if change is to be accepted and successful.[6] Is the dissatisfaction there in the Church? To what extent? Is there recognition of the consequences of just carrying on as we are?

It is the leader's job to help people to see why change needs to happen – to point to the 'burning platform', the urgent need to move from where we are, to encourage the development of the new vision and articulate the organization's identity in such a way as to allow constructive change. Leadership is a critical factor in successful transformation. The purpose of the second part of this book is to suggest a process that will allow those who want to lead change to see it happen.

Part 2
TAKING ACTION

3

Trust the process

The last chapter set out a way of understanding the *components* and *interactions* that make organizations successful over time. This chapter sets out a relatively simple *process* that allows organizations to set about making the changes required to be more successful. It is this process that will determine the structure for the rest of the book.

> ### Cameo 3: Trust the process
> When the Superior General of a religious care organization set out to create a better future for the Sisters and their mission, she realized she was taking them into unknown territory. She was clear that the Sisters were being asked 'to launch out into the deep', well out of their comfort zones. This is how she described it again and again. The Sisters were setting off on a journey without really knowing where it would end or what it would be like on the way. In the event there were many occasions when Sisters became concerned that things were taking too long or, at other times, going too fast. There was too much talk and not enough action or, on the other hand, changes were being made too quickly. Sometimes people wondered if things were going in the right direction or would really make things better. But the Superior General believed the process being followed was the right one and that it had to be seen through to get the right result. Again and again she asked the Sisters to 'trust the process'.

A process for creating sustainable success

Content and ownership

What does this process need to achieve? What would you want it to give you? You need good content; that is, a clear picture of the future and a convincing route to getting there. But you also need some assurance that this future is both realistic and achievable *and* consistent with who you are. Further, you also need to have the Church united behind it, committed to it, energized by it. And you need to know how you are going to implement it. If there is a particular problem (lack of money or a building not fit for purpose or surplus to requirements – both common enough), then of course the strategy needs to solve it.

Traditional approaches to strategy have tended to focus on the *content*. Leaders have used clever people to carry out analyses and propose a way forward. But the best strategies are of no use if they remain on the shelf or only understood and accepted by a few. If strategies are to have any real traction they need to be 'owned' by as many people as possible. The process that follows is designed to create these outcomes.

One of the process's key features is that clarity about who you are and where you are going precedes decisions about organizational change. If you do need to make structural changes, for example, they will be far more effective if they come at the end of the process rather than as the starting point for change. The most important step is creating a commonly understood and accepted picture of what you want the future to look like. It is a mistake to think that organizational problems can be solved by structural changes alone or as the first step – the National Health Service bears eloquent testimony to the limitations of trying to drive performance by such means, where successive reorganizations have failed to achieve the results promised.

Step by step

The process outlined here did not begin with a theory but is the result of reflection upon what actually happens when organizations change effectively. It is summarized thus:

Self-determination and ambition

Effective change starts with one person: someone who is ambitious – not for themselves but for the organization. That person probably does not have a complete or clear vision of the future but knows that it is important to change and is determined to make the change happen. Leadership is critical. The ambitious person will probably be in a leadership role – and the more senior in the organization, the greater his or her capacity to influence the whole organization.

Leadership formation

But this person cannot do it alone. Typically the leader needs to gather a group – a team of people who come to share the ambition. This team will share the load, provide mutual support and model the change required.

Core identity

The team starts by getting some clarity on the organization's identity. It will take time and trouble to articulate its purpose ('Why does the organization exist?') and values ('What is important to us?'; 'What does the organization stand for?') as authentically as possible. These are, if you like, the 'emotional' questions – this is about the soul of the organization.

Vision and strategy

The next step is more rational. The leadership team will go on to develop a vision of the future – the fruit of reflection upon the needs of all those with a stake in the outcome and upon trends in the environment. Through this process the ambition that started the process will begin to take concrete shape. The team will look hard and honestly at the current reality and propose a strategy to get from the present to the future. This is likely to comprise a relatively small number of important initiatives.

Engagement and mobilization

It is now time to involve – to *engage* – a wider circle of people. All the work done up to this point has the status of a hypothesis and is presented as such to everyone in the organization. They are invited to express their views on it, add to it and also consider what it would mean for them if it was substantially adopted.

Depending on the size of the organization this can be quite a major operation, but it is essential if the vision and strategy are to make a real difference.

Alignment

Once the statement of purpose, values, vision and strategy have been finalized, it is time to make it happen. It is at this point that the organization changes processes and systems to support the new direction. The value of those changes is, however, usually overstated – it will be more important to encourage and support different ways of behaving. This may well involve some form of learning and development for individuals.

Renewal

Finally the organization recognizes that the process of creating the future cannot be done once and for all. It must create the capacity to keep learning, keep adapting and renewing itself.

The whole sequence is captured in the model known as 'The Swirl' (see Figure 3.1).

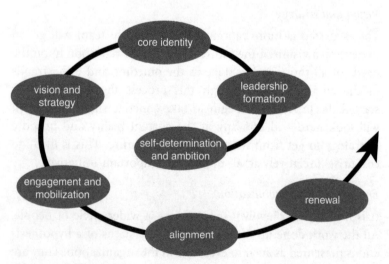

Figure 3.1 The Swirl
Copyright © Telos Partners Limited

Must we do all this?

Cameo 4: A new building

A Methodist church in south London owned some open land in addition to the site on which the church building stood. The church and its halls were dilapidated and out of date. A plan was developed to build a new church and hall on the other site – funded largely from the sale of part of it. The church wanted to ensure there would be sufficient interest in using the new hall from community organizations to bring in income to make the project viable in the years to come. This aspiration was underpinned by an only partly articulated notion of the church's role as a community centre. At first energy was devoted to the purely practical question of identifying potential lets for the new hall. After a while the minister and lay leaders began to realize that this fresh start on a new site posed some rather more fundamental questions to which they did not have complete answers. What is the Church trying to do? What does it stand for? Whom does it want to work with and why? What do we want this community centre to achieve? What do people in the community need? This necessitated a fruitful process of inquiry and discussion that had not been envisaged originally, as well as a certain amount of strategic 'retro-fitting'. The outcome was fine, but it did become evident to all that it might have been better to have started with these questions, not least because it would have influenced building design for the better!

All this may seem a daunting prospect – some may be asking whether it is really all necessary. It promises, in the first place, to take a lot of time and resources and be a somewhat drawn-out affair. The local church, for example, is not a complex organization – does it really require such an apparently elaborate process?

What is already in place?

It can help to think of the process as a jigsaw with a number of pieces. It may be that you have some of the pieces already in place. For example, perhaps you have already done a lot of work to develop a strategy and are happy with the result. You are just not sure it is making any difference or having the impact you had hoped. It may be that you need to focus your efforts on the engagement and alignment phases – do the work that will enable others to both own and influence it and put it into practice. This is fine, so long as the other pieces of the jigsaw really are there.

A particular problem?

Or perhaps you have identified some particular initiatives designed to solve particular problems. Sometimes a discrete fix really is all that is required. But this is usually only the case if the problem is purely practical or pretty small – one that does not have undue emotional significance for the organization. There are not many issues about which all of that can be said, though something like an appeal to restore the church organ might be an example. Emotions might well be involved in this case too, but it may be a sufficiently self-contained and non-controversial issue to be treated on its own.

Let me illustrate the point with an example of something that may not be best dealt with as a discrete issue. Suppose you are a parish short of funds and you decide to address it by launching a stewardship campaign. You have gone straight from a problem (we don't have enough money) to the alignment phase (a stewardship campaign organized). Stewardship campaigns have a tendency to say: 'God has given us all resources. We should use them well and make sure we give an appropriate amount to his work (that is, the local church). We need more money and we would like you to increase the percentage of your income that you give.' This is fine – as far as it goes. Such an appeal will probably have some effect but is unlikely to be transformative. In reality people give to support what they are excited about, what they believe in, what they want to feel part of. If we want to improve giving it will be far more powerful if we are able to put it in a larger context – to say: 'We have a vision that we have created together of what this church will do in the service of Christ. It is something we are all passionate about. It requires our commitment and our resources, so I invite you to help us make it happen.'

We can only do this if we are able to make the links from what we believe in; to what we hope to achieve; to how we plan to get there; and if we have a community that feels ownership of it all. Going straight to discrete solutions may be the right thing to do, but usually only if the answers to the other questions in the process already exist.

It will often help to think about what you have already 'banked' before setting out on the process. The Swirl can be used as a diagnostic to test where you really are. Take each stage and ask: Do we have what is required at this stage already? For example, starting at the beginning: Do we have a leader with ambition for the organization who is prepared to lead us in achieving it? Try using a traffic-light system for each stage: red equals 'not in place'; amber equals 'partly in place'; green equals 'sufficiently in place'. Where lights are green you may be able to move on swiftly to the next stage; where lights are red or amber you will need to spend more time.

Will the Church's culture support this process?

I said earlier that the process described in this book is one that allows an honest conversation to take place between concerned parties. It is this conversation that the Church appears to find difficult – it struggles to manage difference and conflict well. This is hardly a failing unique to the Church of England but it is marked and damaging. A few years' ago I worked with a bishop's staff team that sought – ultimately – to transform the work of the churches of the diocese. The work stalled relatively early on. It was extremely difficult to get real commitment to the process from the team members – one told me later that the issues raised by the work were too close for comfort and that the team was avoiding the conflict that would inevitably arise if all approached it with the honesty and commitment required.

There are many reasons for discomfort with honest disclosure. Clergy work largely alone. Their symbolic role separates them from congregations and they may have few, if any, colleagues with whom to interact day to day. Clergy are the object of a great deal of projection and in the eyes of their congregations are usually either heroes or villains for reasons that have little to do with their actual qualities. The culture of the Church of England puts pressure on them to be saintly all-rounders: there is thus little recognition of real strengths and weaknesses. All of this creates a combination of insecurity and isolation reinforced by clergy members' habitual desire to put on their best faces with one another at chapter meetings and the like. In short, there is no habit of honest, accurate feedback. Interestingly, the Experiences of Ministry Survey 2011 finds that:

> Those reporting highest levels of engagement were most likely to be high in self efficacy (confidence), have a more proactive personality, have been ordained more recently, and have an intellectually challenging role in which they receive useful feedback on how well they are performing and are relatively free to make decisions.[1]

There is a discomfort with admitting we are not perfect, a desire to put on a good show, and it bedevils the Church. It is ironic considering we are supposed to be the body that deals with human imperfections, and one of the reasons why the instinct to cover up scandal is so strong.

At the same time the Church's theological differences are rarely addressed directly. Evangelicals harrumph to Evangelicals, Catholics to Catholics, Liberals to Liberals. Arguments are conducted through books, articles, the letters column of the *Church Times*, through formal synodical process or through grandstanding gestures. It is rare that church people sit down together and talk directly about differences – they are happier lobbing grenades from a distance.

Finding common ground

Are the differences within the Church too great to be overcome? A few years ago one of my colleagues and I were invited to facilitate the formation of one of the new church regional training partnerships (RTPs). These partnerships were intended to develop a strategic approach to the provision of ministerial and other training in designated regions.[2] Our intervention involved bringing all the key players together, in the same room, for a two-day workshop. This was a group of diverse personalities and theologies, many concerned that a 'strategic approach' might threaten their jobs or institutions. The process was ordered but it encouraged people to talk to one another honestly. The first day was predictably sticky, characterized by defensiveness and much marking out of territory. By the end of the second day, however, we had succeeded in getting the group to have a proper conversation. They discovered that they had more in common than they realized and were excited about what they could do together. This RTP is still active and productive – some of the others are not. It is a small but significant example of what can be achieved through straightforward conversation where differences are acknowledged and common ground sought, and where the process encourages less emotive exchanges. The Church needs more of this.

It will never agree on everything and not even, probably, on some pretty fundamental issues – and there is no process or formula that will command everyone's support. That is true in every organization. In businesses the 'refuseniks' would be managed out or managed around. These solutions are not available in the Church of England, so there will always be people who will not 'play'. But it should be possible to gain *sufficient* agreement about common purpose and values to allow a more coherent response to the challenges facing the Church today – one that would be supported by *most*.

One bishop told me that the way the media presents the Church – hopelessly divided; at odds with itself – does not reflect the reality on the ground in his diocese. Actually there is plenty of good will. He has been able to create a simple statement about the direction of the diocese that commands support and inspires confidence and joint action to 'take control' of the future of the Church. This statement is starting to drive everything the diocese does. It describes the purpose of the Church in that diocese as: Going Deeper into God, Transforming Communities and Making New Disciples. As the bishop told me, the Church will never unite by trying to resolve different views on women bishops or gay clergy. What it needs is to focus on is its vision of God and his work. That is what will inspire the energy and action required to create a more hopeful future.

4

Get on the 'T'

My colleagues and I have found again and again that positive organizational change begins with a leader. The root is not an idea, but a person. This leader is a person of exceptional ambition, belief and determination. He or she has a conviction about the need for change, about the scale of the change required and believes it can – or must – be brought about. Quite often this person cannot see the way clearly but is determined to set out on the journey nonetheless. One client told me: 'I didn't know what we needed to do but I knew we had to do something.' A transformation that is securing the future of a 150-year-old organization began with that conviction.

This chapter describes the role of the leader in initiating and anchoring effective positive organizational change, and some features of contemporary thinking about the role and qualities of effective leaders. It suggests a process of reflection for leaders designed to help them identify their own ambition and priorities. Finally, it addresses concerns about the language and role of leadership that I have observed in the Church.

Cameo 5: Out of your comfort zone

The chief executive of an engineering business complained of being forced into too much of the daily operational activity in his business. This prevented him from giving attention to long-term strategy and to the sales and networking his role required. In particular he was drawn into the management of the company finances. We explored this problem for a number of coaching sessions! Was the finance director not up to the job? He was, but had too much to do. Could the CEO perhaps add someone to the finance team to spread the load?

> Possible. What would that cost? £35,000 a year. What additional revenue would be generated by the CEO giving his focus to sales and networking? £500,000 a year. Looks like a no-brainer then? But still the CEO struggled to get out of the finances and into the CEO role as he believed it should be. Eventually he stumbled on the truth. He had been a finance director, knew the job and felt comfortable in it. The CEO's job involved going a long way out of his comfort zone and he was struggling to embrace it.

The role of the leader is to be the tireless advocate of change. Then he or she must create the conditions and guide a process in the organization that allows the change to be explored and more fully articulated, others to be enrolled and the necessary planning and action to take place.

This is all true in a particular way of the strategic development activity that is the subject of this book, but in fact it is always the role of the leader. It is easy to talk of 'leading change' as if it is a particular aspect of leadership or a task that becomes necessary from time to time. In fact to lead is to lead change – that is the role. Organizations cannot stand still without slipping back – they have to adapt continually to external changes. The leader – at every level in an organization – stands at the junction of the three functions of leadership captured in the Trialogue (see Chapter 2), helping the organization make the right choices about the future while managing today's business. The change involved may be designed to improve the day-to-day operation (its 'efficiency') or to fit it better to meet the new demands of the changing environment (its 'effectiveness').

What qualities and skills might leaders need? What kind of things might they do to be effective?

The leader

On many occasions I have asked groups to reflect on their experience of being led and to consider what good leaders do and what qualities they possess. The answers given by one group are entirely typical. First, to the question 'What do good leaders do?'

- inspire confidence;
- trust you;
- listen – to ideas and so on;
- add own ideas;
- value other voices;
- treat everyone equally;
- lead by example – role modelling;
- look at the problem;
- set objectives;
- give clear direction;
- be available, approachable;
- be able to make a decision;
- be flexible.

Second, to the question 'What qualities do good leaders possess?'

- confidence;
- integrity;
- courage;
- fairness, justness;
- honesty;
- empathy;
- real caring;
- clarity;
- conviction;
- tolerance.

I usually start here so that I can use the ideas of contemporary writers on leadership to augment and confirm what most people already know! I find it interesting to note what the groups *never* say about good leaders:

- are especially clever;
- have all the answers;
- tell us what to do.

Traditional thinking on leadership emphasized 'command and control' (leaders know what to do and tell you how to do it), a form that may have suited the early days of industrial mass production. It may work in organizations such as the army, though the army recognizes more readily than most the need to lead in a way that builds teams that utilize the skills of all and release 'discretionary effort'. Today the need to engage people's skills and commitment is so evident that thinking about leadership has shifted well away from command and control, and also from notions of charisma and heroism. This may come as a relief to many in leadership positions. The titles of these recent books say it all:

Transformational Leadership
Servant Leadership
Inspiring Leadership
Resonant Leadership
Emotionally Intelligent Leadership
Authentic Leadership[1]

As they imply, leadership is a popular subject today, and while there are many subtle variations captured in the literature, there are common themes. We might summarize the thinking by saying that good leaders need interpersonal skills and the ability to create a purposeful framework for action while empowering people to act and contribute their own skills. Ideally, leaders are highly determined, focused people who do not make it happen by themselves but work with and through others. Here is a list of leadership competencies derived from Robert Greenleaf's work:

- listening and understanding;
- acceptance and empathy;
- intuition;
- foresight;
- awareness and perception;
- thinking long term.[2]

Above all, perhaps, personal integrity and authenticity are vital. This is important because there is a sense in which the new ideas about leadership are as daunting as the old ones. Once you needed to know all the answers; now you need exemplary interpersonal skills. Who are these paragons of emotional intelligence and empowering action? The point about authenticity seems to imply that leaders who are not such paragons can be successful if they are seen to 'be themselves', to have a genuine commitment to something that others value, even if they make mistakes or are sometimes, in emotional intelligence terms, a little inept.

In the end it is difficult to say exactly what good leadership is. Most people seem to know it when they see it, but defining it satisfactorily is another matter. St Peter would not have met either the old or the new criteria particularly well. Perhaps people have to be good leaders 'in their own way' rather than conform to any model. Maybe what we need is 'good enough' leadership. Can anyone be a leader? It is true, probably, that some are born with qualities that help, but it is equally true that everyone can improve their leadership skills by deepening their understanding of the task and developing the ability to manage themselves and others.

The task of leadership

Leadership and the Trialogue

Much writing has been devoted to describing and distinguishing between 'management' and 'leadership'. Managers keep the show on the road while leaders blaze the trail to pastures new. The distinction provides helpful insights, but the Trialogue gives a more complete and elegant solution. The proposition is simply that the role of the leader is to mediate the three-way conversation between managing the present, creating the future and nurturing identity. Managing the present roughly conforms to what some describe as 'management' and creating the future to 'leadership'. Nurturing identity is the additional factor and should influence both present and future activity.

Leadership at the right level

The more senior[3] you are the more focus you should put on creating the future and nurturing identity. One of the key challenges of leadership is that of operating at the right level. Successful leaders do not allow themselves to become too 'operational' – that is, drawn too much into the doing. Leadership is not administration, nor is it having all the answers. On the other hand, leaders cannot abdicate responsibility or remain *too much* above the fray. In most organizations, leaders do get too involved in operations – the temptation is to micro-manage. In the Church of England, however, there are bishops who would much prefer the organization to manage itself entirely. The choice should not be between doing everything and staying above the action. The role of strategic leadership is to create the environment, set the context and ensure there is a framework for taking action. It does not seek to do all the work but to lead the process and ensure it is done – it sets the pace, initiates work to establish the direction and has oversight of the work that follows. The execution of this requires commitment, courage and an ability to work with other people.

Leadership and the Church

The words used in this chapter – 'leader', 'ambition' – are problematic for many, especially in church circles. They may well be heard as an unwelcome intrusion from the world of business or politics and seen as bringing with them notions such as ruthlessness, preoccupation with worldly success, self-aggrandizement, ego and superficiality. But while it is true that all these qualities can indeed be found in abundance in the business world (and in almost all organizations, including the Church!), they are not, it should now be clear, what is being recommended.

Ambition here does not mean ambition for self but rather for the organization. It could be characterized as a sense of calling or vocation. In the church context one might ask instead: 'What is God calling me to do?' And leadership does not refer to charismatic individuals operating by force of personality nor dictators ruling by personal fiat. This is not about a heroic leader single-handedly building a road to the future. We are not talking about people who know it all. On the contrary, we are talking about people who know they cannot do it alone, can work with others and are willing to subordinate themselves to the larger cause.

The most effective businessmen are not celebrities – you will probably not have heard of most of them, nor will you see them on TV programmes such as *The Apprentice*, which promote and pander to the least attractive features of the business world.

The Church, theology and leadership

Why is there so much resistance to the language of leadership? Perhaps it is because many see it as secular in origin and a manifestation of 'management speak'. And if that's right, behind it may lie a concern that leadership or management language is incompatible with the sacred nature of priesthood – an understandable point of view, but based on a misunderstanding of the best of the leadership thinkers and writers. There is nothing incompatible with Christianity about most current leadership theory, as the earlier part of this chapter should have helped to make clear. It is also worth noting that in the UK, the study of leadership has been profoundly influenced by Christians such as John Adair.

Furthermore, there is no essential incompatibility between modern views on leadership and Anglican ecclesiology. Although priesthood and episcopacy are rich concepts with much more to them than the elements of leadership I have emphasized, it is hard to see how vicars or bishops could deny the leadership dimension of their tasks. I have acknowledged the unattractive nature of 'management speak' but am just as concerned by 'theology speak', which is too often deployed to avoid the reality and challenge of leadership and to kick the issue into the long grass. The principal challenge of leadership is not defining or theologizing about it, but doing it, and 'leadership' here means something far richer than the management stereotype. Some may still need convincing, but the theological and spiritual questions are best answered as we go along, rather than we refuse to move until they are all resolved to everyone's satisfaction – anything else is a recipe for inaction.

So returning to the Trialogue: this describes the three key activities of the viable or adaptive organization. Leadership does not reside in any one of these three but at their intersection – and the role of leadership is to manage the tension between these three imperatives.

Are the functions captured in the Trialogue so different from those of Christian ministry? In 2009, the Senior Appointments

Group (Episcopal) presented a paper to the College of Bishops describing episcopal roles.[4] This presented a model of episcopacy that has a great deal in common with the Trialogue, a 'secular' product. The roles were described as:

1 priest – signifier concerned with being and purpose;
2 prophet – disturber concerned with seeing new possibilities and raising expectancy;
3 apostolic leader – transformer concerned with doing, with revealing the kingdom in the present;
4 theologian – reflector concerned with thinking, with interpretation.

One could quite convincingly see the role of priest in terms of nurturing identity, of the prophet as creating the future and the apostolic leader as managing the present. The theologian, the thinker, could be seen as the equivalent of the interpretative role of the leader at the intersection of the Trialogue.

Not everyone was convinced by this model of episcopal leadership but, set alongside the Trialogue, it demonstrates that there is a richness in both ecclesiastical and secular reflection on the role – or roles – of leaders as well as recurring themes. The Church may need convincing that secular ideas about leadership have sufficient subtlety or weight. In fact contemporary thinking about organizations and leadership owes an immense debt to the Christian tradition, and one would expect the Church to be more receptive to it than it sometimes is.

Defining the leadership role in the Church

One of the challenges facing the Church is that the role of its leaders is contested and ill-defined. Bishops all define their roles differently. One might see himself as a theologian, another as a leader of mission, another as a community leader. These are not just described as personal preferences reflecting different gifts but are usually presented as a matter of religious principle, as the outworking of a sacred model of episcopacy. There is no arguing with assertions presented in this way!

Of course the role of a bishop includes all the features mentioned in the previous paragraph, and it is this, among other things, that makes the job so difficult. But it appears that many bishops tend to restrict their leadership to the personal, community or academic spheres. Strategic leadership is much less well understood, and bishops are less well prepared for it. Some deal with this by leaving the job to someone else. A team from the bishop's council might be set up to develop strategy, thus delegating a fundamental leadership activity to a committee. The problem is that if a leader vacates a space, someone else will fill it, and this will frequently be the diocesan secretary. These are admirable and capable people but they cannot provide strategic leadership – a bishop *has* to occupy this space whatever else he might do. It is at the heart of the role.

A similar confusion exists at parish level, where clergy sometimes see themselves as pastors, teachers or missioners rather than leaders – many describe themselves as priests *as against* leaders or managers. All ordained Anglicans are priests and have a ministry given by God and the Church to care for God's people, celebrate the sacraments and represent the gospel in the world. Some may have more gifts and a greater sense of calling in a particular aspect of this basic vocation. But many priests are also incumbents of parishes, deans of cathedrals or bishops of dioceses – and this brings with it a leadership role in the Church. This is reinforced by the reality that the stipendiary parish priest is becoming more like a local bishop with several churches to lead, supported by non-stipendiary priests and lay people who 'do' the regular work of leading services, visiting the sick and so forth. Many priests are struggling to understand what their changing role means or how to do it. For many a more strategic leadership role is hard to grasp – it is easier and more congenial to immerse oneself in the doing. This is a recipe for burnout in multi-parish benefices.

All organizations require leadership, and in the Church of England it is a role given to the clergy. Most clergy, of course, accept this. They do not usually receive training that recognizes it, though dioceses are increasingly responding to this need. The clergy must be equipped to lead the Church in a way that is realistic about how the role of stipendiary ministry is developing in the modern Church of England.

The process for the individual

If effective and sustainable change starts with the ambition of a single leader, then the proper activity for those in leadership or coming into it is to undertake a process of personal reflection intended to help them decide how best to occupy their role. This process should help the leader to think about both 'me' and 'me in this role'. Leaders need to ask themselves how they see their role, what is important to them, what they are here for, what God is calling them to. Leaders do not need to be perfect, thank God, but they need to know themselves. They also need to know what they are trying to achieve – they need a vision and they need to commit themselves to it.

Again, I have found it helpful to use the Trialogue here. It provides as good a framework for the 'viable individual' as for the viable organization. Below, under the three headings of the Trialogue, are some questions you might consider.

Nurturing identity

- What is important to me?
- What are my values?
- What (if any) tensions exist for me as a leader of this organization?
- How will I act in such a way as to remain true to myself while serving the Church?
- What are the strengths I should build on? What personal skills and awareness do I need to develop to be more effective? How do I need to lead?

Creating the future

- Where do I want to be/go in the future?
- What are my aspirations for the church I lead?
- How willing am I to lead the church in addressing its challenges and realizing its opportunities?
- What tensions are created for me by the prospect of change (personally and organizationally)?

Managing the present

- What roles do I perform?
- How do I understand the role of leadership alongside other personal and professional roles?
- How do I balance my energies?
- What tensions are there in balancing my roles and energies?

Clergy will probably have considered these things already but it helps to keep them under review. It would be very useful to do this explicitly during the transition into a new appointment. And having answered the questions, leaders might start to develop personal strategies for achieving the desired goals for the organization, *and* for obtaining the necessary support and managing the tensions that will inevitably arise for them as individuals.

This is in part about the personal cost of leadership. It takes immense amounts of time and energy and can be painful, particularly if it involves challenging the organization – as it really must. How is one to manage other important roles such as being a wife or husband? Ideally there will be some way of achieving balance, some way leaders can nourish themselves and manage other roles and responsibilities.[5]

The stress here is on the importance of preparing for new roles and of the early months in a new appointment. One of the better features of the Church of England is that it does offer people space of this kind and is not in a tearing hurry to see results. Both incumbents and bishops have time to think in the early stages – and to listen. If one is to be ambitious for a new organization one needs some time for discernment. New bishops, for example, ought to recognize the 'step up' they are being asked to take – however experienced and able you are, such a change of responsibility puts you right back into the role of learner. Fortunately, help is more available these days and funds are available for coaches – someone who will support you through the process of thought and planning required. Leaders will benefit from all available help and should reject any sense that they should not need it – after all, Roger Federer has a coach.

But I also wish to underline the urgency inherent in the leadership task. There is a tendency, described to me recently by one bishop, to come into role thinking that not a great deal needs to be done because the diocese is not in obvious difficulty. Those appointed later in life may be disposed to see themselves as having a relatively short tenure in which the priority is to provide a steady hand on the tiller. This is not a good pattern. First, no organization can opt for steady as she goes. Organizations are either moving forward or dropping back – there is no other option. Second, the Church of England is nowhere in a condition where creating the future is not an urgent priority. It is good for leaders not to be too quick to act when new in post unless there is a real emergency. But leaders are most able to think new thoughts and engage others in action earlier in their time in office. They should spend time getting to know people and situations but need to signal their intentions early and act on them within the first year.

Summary of actions

Essentially I am recommending a process of observation, thought, questioning and personal reflection.

1 Consider how you can best undertake the leadership role.
2 Understand what that role demands of you as a person.
3 Discover the needs of the organization you serve.
4 Articulate your ambition for the Church and commit yourself to it.
5 Identify the help you need.

5

Create a team

Successful change starts with an individual but individuals cannot do it by themselves. They need to share the leadership. Good leaders are not geniuses with a thousand helpers but people who work with and through others. Ambitious ones need teams that will share the ambition and the task of turning it into reality.

So much has been written and said about teamworking that it is hard to believe there are many in leadership who do not have some understanding of the principles involved. While there is no need to repeat much of it here, this chapter will consider why teamworking is important and underline the key factors in building a successful team. It will then explore some of the issues and questions that may arise when applying these ideas in the Church of England – in particular why it appears to struggle to create real teamworking. Finally, it will offer some practical suggestions for selecting and building an effective team.

> ### Cameo 6: Becoming a real team
>
> A hospital had been working hard for two years to achieve the level of performance required to become a foundation trust. During that period there had been progress but it was patchy and insufficient. Things started to change when the leadership team began to work differently, spending considerable time working on themselves. They became much more explicit in their understanding of what the role of the team and of the individuals in it should be. They thought about how they worked with one another and with those who reported to them. They started to be more honest with one another and to get to know one another at a deeper level. They acknowledged the strengths and weaknesses of the team and made plans to address the

weaknesses. Above all they became a great deal clearer on what the team had to do to make change happen. A key shift was moving from a sense of the team as a group that came together to coordinate activities for which individuals had responsibilities – finance, HR, operations and so forth – to a sense of it as a group of people who had a shared responsibility for the success of the hospital, a shared commitment to achieving the overall outcome. The team went on to lead a pioneering integration of health and social care services in their county.

What teams can give you

What do we really mean by a team and what is it designed to deliver? It seems evident that an ambitious leader will benefit from sharing the load, that two heads are better than one. But the value of a team can and perhaps should be greater than that. The best teams offer a whole greater than the sum of the parts – they can create an impact far greater than the combined actions of the individuals. If you are trying to effect a transformation this is a huge and probably necessary asset. On the other hand, if what you are trying to do is merely keep it steady as she goes, you probably do not need it.

Leaders who wish to see a significant change for the better in the effectiveness of the Church will not be able to do it on their own and will need to be able to create and manage teams well. A team may have flaws but it must share the ambition of the leader to create that new future. Given that the team is likely to be inherited it may well be necessary to make the case for change to the team ahead of anyone else.

What is a team?

It is useful to distinguish the team from a committee or steering group. The latter have their place but are not very helpful when you want to make a big difference to an organization. Such groups typically work slowly, emphasize process and tend to coordinate a number of essentially individual contributions. They are fundamentally bureaucratic – good for maintaining and managing tried and tested processes.

The team is an anti-bureaucratic concept. Teams are focused on the outcome – this is what drives them to do things together rather than separately. Of course members of the team have particular areas of responsibility, but they are not jealous of these and see the whole task as the primary focus. They tend to keep the processes to the minimum required to ensure that things are done in an organized fashion. They favour pace and seek to maintain momentum, doing what they need to do to 'make it happen'. It is in working like this that they manifest corporate qualities that exceed the sum of their individual gifts.

Katzenbach and Smith[1] carried out research that concluded that effective teams are not formed by the belief that teamworking is a good thing but by commitment to a shared objective that manifests itself as a shared task. If this does not exist, all the team-building in the world will avail little – the members may all get on nicely but at a superficial level, and it will be a team only in a limited sense. Effectiveness for a team is directly connected to the strength of the shared sense of purpose and commitment to the objectives.

The experience of teams

While teams can be enormously powerful, there is a danger of idealizing them. Perhaps all the talk of teams has created a rather sentimental notion – do we nurture some idea of them as places of harmonious relationships, constant honesty, profound bonding, seamless effectiveness? In fact it is rarely, if ever, like that – idealizing teams may prevent us getting the best from them.

Teams have different characters and quirks. The inside story of a number of successful sports teams shows that it is not essential that everyone be best friends or even like one another that much. Teams can be argumentative, uncomfortable places. We will have to manage them our own way and perhaps not too idealistically. For a team engaged in leading an organization, the most important ingredient is the common commitment to realizing the ambition for that organization.

Teamworking in the Church

There is a great deal of emphasis on 'teams' in the Church of England, but on the whole it is not particularly good at them. There seem to be two principal reasons.

A culture of individualism

The first is the habitual attitudes of the clergy – though this may be changing as more people with experience of working in team-orientated environments are ordained. Nevertheless many clergy are individualists – often rather self-consciously maverick – working with a model of priesthood that sets them apart from others. The model is still, in practice, that of the omnicompetent priest with some helpers, and further isolation then ensues from the pressures of that role. There is a vicious circle here: the role isolates people, which in turn magnifies the common clerical anxiety about how well they are doing and how they are seen, which in turn further magnifies the tendency to isolation.

A lack of shared purpose

The second and biggest reason why teamworking is less effective than it could be is the failure to establish common purpose and common goals – the deficiencies in teamworking are a direct consequence of not thinking strategically about the Church, not clearly articulating what it is trying to achieve. In these days of multi-parish benefices and groups in which stipendiary clergy *have* to lead the efforts of a larger team of laypeople and self-supporting clergy, these omissions will have to be addressed.

Creating an effective team

I once asked my colleague Alan Davies what he had learnt about teamworking from his experience in the 1990s of coaching Wales to the Five Nations Rugby Championship. He said it helped a lot if you chose the right team in the first place. We read that Jesus began his transformative ministry by selecting a team of twelve to work with him – his example encourages us to believe that the right team might not necessarily be composed of obvious choices or 'star players'.

So the first step is selecting the right team. Of course, in practice few leaders have the luxury of picking a new team from scratch, but even where there is an inherited group, it may be possible to change it. What criteria should be employed in selection? It is helpful to think about this because it provides the basis of a challenge to inherited teams.

Who is in the team? The ideal

1 Since the first and most important quality is commitment to the ambition, the leader should be sounding out candidates to see who shares the desire to make the kind of difference required.
2 The team should be composed of people who want to work together, *as a team*, to achieve the desired outcome. Star players should be brought on board if possible but not at the expense of the team.
3 Team members probably need to have some kind of legitimacy in the organization. This means choosing from those who occupy recognized and relevant positions or are seen to have qualities and qualifications that fit them for the role.
4 The team should be a group of people who are willing to accept responsibility, individually and jointly, to take the action required to lead the realization of the ambition.
5 Finally, team members need to accept that organizational change starts with them, and that their willingness and ability to model the change will be an essential ingredient in a succesful project.

If teams are to work closely together and share responsibility, they should not be so large that a committee or steering-group approach becomes inevitable. Six to nine is probably the ideal number, even if there is good authority for going as high as twelve.

Who is in the team? The reality

In the case of the bishop the team will likely be the 'bishop's staff meeting'. This team includes, typically, suffragan bishops, archdeacons, dean of the cathedral, diocesan secretary and perhaps heads of diocesan departments. Ideally the team will be selected by the bishop along the lines suggested above, but that is a luxury rarely if ever available in practice. Everybody inherits a team and has limited power to change it except over time. The secular chief executive can generally move quite swiftly, but the problem in the Church is that the time period is likely to be years. This makes it all the more important to invest time early in developing a shared vision and objectives and a way of working, which will require a willingness to face up to difference and conflict openly and honestly, even though the temptation may be to avoid it. This work should be based on a shared sense of the change required. Following Gleicher again[2] (see p. 33), the leader will need to be able to articulate clearly why change is required, what the better future might look like – to the extent he or she can at this stage – and what steps might be taken to move in the right direction.

In the case of the parish priest – whether the incumbent of a single parish or team rector – the position is less predictable and there may be more flexibility and discretion. The team should include staff – where there are some! Other clergy, readers and wardens are the obvious candidates but the incumbent should consider who the key people are and try to include them. As already suggested, it is wise to involve people who enjoy credibility and respect – even if they are difficult, it may be better to have them *inside* the tent! But remember too that attitude and commitment are ultimately more important than experience and ability. Judgement is required here – if you are in a position to choose the team, it may be the most important decision you make!

The team needs to be a group of people with, or willing to accept, real responsibility – not a committee of advisers. PCCs, diocesan synods and bishops' councils cannot play this role, though they are a critical part of the overall picture. The team needs to be a gathering of the 'executive', not those with governance roles. Who are the people who will help you 'make it happen'?

Getting off to a good start

It is said that the most effective teams do not spend a great deal of their time focusing on their internal relationships but rather on the task, but they can do this because they invested time early in the life of the team establishing the personal and social relationships positively. The leader will have to model and insist on this until it becomes a true group norm, but if positive behavioural habits are instilled early on, the benefits are great in the long term. This might include, for example, the exchange of honest feedback referred to earlier. Good feedback is offered positively and is intended to improve another person's confidence and performance. It is driven by a concern to see the other and the team succeed, and teams operate most effectively where this is the accepted norm. It makes learning and improvement fundamental to the way the team works.

So the team needs to start by working on itself. Once created, it needs to spend time, early and deliberately, establishing its identity – its understanding of itself, its role and way of working. What will this look like? It requires dedicated time spent addressing these issues in workshop style, perhaps with external facilitation. For those who want to get on with it, this might seem unnecessary – a distracting preliminary where problems are urgent. But the success of most ventures is determined in the set-up – sometimes you have to go slow to go fast. If you get the foundation right you can address the issues with far greater purpose and despatch – time given to preparation allows the athlete to race away on the very 'B' of 'Bang'.

The task is even more urgent if a team is inherited rather than chosen, because it will probably have established deeply engrained group norms – largely unconscious, mostly accidental and, perhaps, unhelpful. All groups have norms – the issue is how positive or otherwise they are. This must be addressed early and thoroughly, even though it will probably be difficult. It is better not to leave any of this to chance.

The best way of facilitating this team-building work is to start with an open conversation about how the team should operate.

A simple vehicle for this is the creation of a 'team charter'. At a minimum the charter should cover:

- The team's purpose – clarity here is the most important issue by far.
- What it expects future success to look like – what the team and its work will look like if it is achieving its purpose.
- The team's values and the behaviour expected of all members.
- The roles that individuals will play in pursuit of the common goals.
- Basic operational practices such as meeting schedules, managing of agendas and so forth.

This charter will need to be reviewed from time to time as it is tested by experience.

Becoming effective

Teams have a typical life cycle of the kind described by Tuckman[3] as: forming, storming, norming and performing (there are many versions of the same essential idea of teams' development stages). Effective teams manage and accelerate the journey through the first three stages and get to the performing stage. In the forming stage they are tentative and polite, needing directive leadership. In the storming stage – often prompted by some kind of crisis or pressure – people start setting out their stall, perhaps rebelling and vying for position. This can be uncomfortable or even explosive but it is natural and necessary – cards need to be on the table and the honest conversation is what is required. In the norming stage the team is clarifying its objectives, roles and ways of working. Expect to see these stages unfolding and attempt to manage and accelerate them.

In the programmes we run with clients we frequently set up activities that involve working in teams, intended to allow learning about team dynamics and team development. Quite often we find that teams believe they are performing well in the early stages – everyone seems to be getting on and the job is being done at least reasonably well – but in fact members are often just being polite to one another. In one programme we set up an elaborate simulation that divided the 50 or so participants into teams charged with competing to establish favourable business relationships with a company board played by actors. Everyone was relaxed about it for the first two days, many not that engaged with or serious about it. On the fourth day each team was scheduled to make a presentation to the fictional clients while observed by all the other teams. By the night before the presentation the relaxed attitudes had gone, the competitive spirit was fully aroused and the pressure on. At this point – and we ran the programme ten times – pretty well every team had some sort of row or episode of storming – the gloves came off, the truth was told and the team dynamic changed. This is normal, and if managed well can allow the team to truly perform.

It is easier to establish a new team than reform an existing one. If you become the leader of an existing team you have quite a complex task. You have to become a member of the team and be accepted – in general you have to be included in a group before you can influence it. This argues against being too demanding or commanding early on. But it is also true that when the membership of a team changes, the team reverts to the forming stage to some degree and will look to the leader for direction. Herein lies an opportunity to encourage a conversation about re-forming the team around a different purpose and/or more positive norms, which may be difficult and involve time and some storming. Team members may seem to be onside and the group working well, but it is worth repeating that in the forming stage this may be illusory or superficial. The truth may take a while to emerge, may only come out under pressure and may be painful to deal with. The more honest the conversation from the start the better, and the leader will need to manage that in a way that is also aware of his or her status as newcomer.

Team work is an exercise in managing our differences and using them to create that whole greater than the sum of its parts. Differences should not be covered up or denied but groups should focus on finding the common ground. Members would do well to cultivate the habit of listening and understanding rather than defending – though in the Church of England the greater danger may be the temptation to avoid or seek too easy and facile an agreement. Decisions that arise from thrashing through conflicting views tend to be sounder than those produced from an easy consensus.

The role of the team is to translate an ambition for the organization into a vision and strategy. It will oversee the process of engaging the organization with the product of its deliberations and ultimately will provide the energy and leadership required to effect any changes. But the task begins with articulating the core identity of the organization.

In the Church, as elsewhere, as the team begins to develop a proposal about the identity and future of its part of the Church, it should give consideration to how it will describe to others what it is doing. People will soon realize that something is happening, which may generate anxiety. Typically people fear that a new strategy will result in painful changes. It is better to tell them frankly what you are doing and be crystal clear that they will have an opportunity to contribute and be heard before anything is decided. It is important to agree a set of 'key messages' that the team will give in answer to likely questions, and these need to be communicated consistently – inconsistency or contradictions will do a great deal of damage to the change process and to the team's authority and credibility.

Summary of actions

1 Decide who is in the team.
2 Ensure – to the extent possible – that you share ambition and commitment to the process of achieving that ambition.
3 Clarify the purpose, objectives, roles and ways of working (the charter).
4 Actively build the team so that it reaches the performing stage and relies less on your leadership.

6

Know who you are

After establishing itself, the first task for the leadership team is to create a hypothesis about the identity of the part of the Church for which the team carries responsibility. As will become more apparent, the word 'hypothesis' is critical. The team is not solving the problem of identity but initiating and informing a conversation that should, in time, embrace all those with a stake in the conclusion.

This chapter describes the key components of identity and its relation to the larger concept of culture, and shows why understanding and rearticulating these is essential to sustainable change. It addresses further the contested nature of identity in the Church of England and argues that the revitalization of its culture is essential for the creation of a better future. Finally, it sets out a process for exploring and redefining purpose and values.

Cameo 7: Reconnecting with purpose

Interesting things happen when we look anew at identity. This was the first thing the General Council of the Roman Catholic Congregation (see p. 37) did when they started out on their journey of change. For years the Congregation's ministry had been to the elderly and children. We re-read some of its foundational statements, notably the constitutions, but discovered no specific mention of either. The mission of the Congregation was simply described as to 'the poor'. It was remembered that the foundress had cared for a wider range of needy people. All this had the liberating effect of releasing the Council from the assumption that the maintenance of its care homes was the prime imperative. Although the decision was quickly taken to retain the core business of providing residential care for the elderly, the Congregation is now also encouraging a positive conversation in its regions about new ministries.

Identity is critical

Why do you do what you do? What gets you up in the morning? Why do you get angry about things, things in the Church, perhaps? Why do you feel so happy at other times about something that has happened in church? It is well worth asking and answering these questions, individually and together.

For example, I am motivated by my passionate belief that we live in God's world, one world, and my desire to make sense of it and help others do the same. This in turn rests on a set of beliefs and experiences that define a Christian faith and life. So one of the main things that gets me up in the morning is the motivating power of this sense of purpose. Our emotional reactions about what happens in the Church – and anywhere else – are powered by our sense of what is right; that is, of the values to which we are committed. We are all in the Church because, however different we may be in many ways, we share a sense of purpose and certain values – not entirely, but enough to join together and share an identity.

The most important factor in reviving a struggling organization is reconnecting with its purpose – that has more renewing power than anything else. Organizations, like teams, are created and defined by a sense of existing for a reason and of standing for certain things – this is what gives them identity and what leads people to create or join them.

Purpose and values

'Purpose' means our objective at the highest level, the thing that will always be there to guide and drive us. NASA, for example, defines its purpose as 'increasing man's capability to explore the heavens'. The Church might talk about 'revealing the kingdom of

God' or 'making known the love of God' or 'following Christ' –
these are definitions of purpose that are large and inexhaustible.
'Values' means the core beliefs and principles that guide us in the
fulfilment of our purpose.

Several studies[1] have suggested that the most successful organizations are clear on their purpose and values and insist on living
them out even at a cost to short-term financial gain. These are
core commitments that cannot be compromised except at grave
cost to the organization.

Identity and change

Nurturing the sense of identity is critical to the organization's
health and success. How are we to make the right choices about
the future? We need to understand the environment we operate
in as best we can and understand how it is changing. There needs
to be rational deliberation about how to be more effective in
the changing world, but any choices we make must be consistent
with who we are and what we stand for – indeed, they must
enable us to be ourselves better and more effectively in that changing world.

If we want to change things we must start by clarifying, articulating and if necessary reclaiming our identity. We need to be able
to set out our purpose and values – the unchanging commitments
that define us and guide everything we do. In the first instance
this is a task for the leadership team.

It is the organization's identity that motivates and engages its
audience – its staff, its customers – or its congregations. Anything
that seems to threaten that identity will cause an emotional reaction and be resisted. If it is compromised, motivation and loyalty
will be damaged and perhaps lost altogether. It will be hard to
create change, however appropriate and well-conceived, without
being able to demonstrate that the new way of doing things
will enable us to be the Church equally authentically but more
effectively. The organization that attempts to build its future in a
way at odds with its identity risks failing. The parish church may
well solve its problems of finance and attendance by converting
to a nightclub but it will probably have made a fatal compromise.

This may seem obvious, but though the stakes are often more subtle, they can be equally significant.

Identity is not a simple issue. Over time purpose and values – the unchanging core – accrete layers of habit and custom that become confused with the core in many minds. Perhaps I want to replace the pews in the local church. This will, to many, appear to threaten the church's identity. Such threats – which in the end are perceived as threats to the values of the individuals concerned – may be quite fiercely resisted. To make the case for such an action I would do well not to appeal to questions of comfort, aesthetics or utility but to show that the new pews or chairs will allow us to pursue the mission and worship of the church more effectively.

The accretions of habit and custom grow quickly in the Church. When I was a parish priest we introduced a donkey to the procession on Palm Sunday – despite reservations from some, mainly focused on concerns about what it might do when we got it into the church. These fears proved largely unfounded, though reassurance was provided in the form of a handler with bucket and shovel. In fact it went so well we repeated it the next year, but in the third year – in a rather high-handed way, without consultation – I decided we'd had the donkey experience, and left it out. There were complaints – 'But we always have a donkey.'

Authenticity is vital

At the time of writing, the Leveson inquiry is still fresh in the mind. It investigated the conduct of Rupert Murdoch's News International in the wake of the phone-hacking scandal and its associated allegations that journalists from the *News of the World* used bribery to obtain information from the police. The inquiry demonstrated just how badly wrong some sections of News International had gone. To many it is confirmation of what they always suspected and a rather enjoyable vindication of a long-held suspicion. But consider this statement: 'The Company expects that every employee, at every level, will strive to conduct himself or herself with integrity.'[2]

This simple statement of values is part of a much longer exposition of the principles on which News Corporation, News

International's parent organization, says it conducts its business. No one can be sure whether these values are genuinely held and have now been compromised, or never were held. What is clear is that organizations get into trouble when they lose sight of their purpose and values or espouse values to which they are not truly committed. Understandably the proliferation of statements like these provokes cynicism when so many fail to live up to the fine way they present themselves.

Values are no use as window dressing. Purpose and values as described here are emphatically *not* nice statements on the office walls and the website but foundational principles doggedly adhered to, even when it does not seem to make business sense. Authenticity is vital.

The task of defining identity

At one level defining identity is a simple enough activity. It is about answering two straightforward questions: 'What are we here for' and 'What are the beliefs and principles that guide us in living out our purpose?' It will be necessary, however, to undertake the enquiry in a way that allows sufficient thought, depth and authenticity. The task here is not to identify what we aspire to so much as what we actually believe and have at least a measure of commitment to. We all fail to live up to our principles, so we do not need to be *perfect* exemplars of our values to hold them truly. On the other hand, we cannot approach the question by compiling a wish list – by deciding what we ought to believe or what will look good in our publicity material. The espoused values need to be our real values or they will merely provoke cynicism.

The requirement for authenticity means that the conversations about identity are often profound, revealing and challenging. The honest conversation may well reveal the organization's dark side as well as its best self. This is a marvellous opportunity to address those destructive tendencies that usually go unacknowledged. For example, in the course of a conversation about its values, one organization admitted that it in fact prized and encouraged greed – it was the principle underpinning its entire reward system. It could decide either to validate or counter it, and it chose the former. Thus a local church may, for example, be forced to confront the reality that while it is theoretically committed to welcoming outsiders, what it actually values is the familiar, club-like atmosphere of a closed group.

Identity and culture

What we are doing here is beginning to open up the question of the organization's culture. By clarifying identity we may bring some of the contradictions that inform the Church's culture into the light, into the conscious. We may also highlight other hidden factors that influence our behaviour and the way we 'show up'. The culture of an organization is the combination of values, assumptions, attitudes, behaviours, processes and 'artefacts' – buildings and all physical manifestations of the organization – that characterize it (see Figure 6.1). Culture pervades, and is manifested in, every aspect. It is extraordinarily powerful and persistent, and its power lies to a large extent in that a great deal of it is unconscious – like an iceberg, most of it is under water. We can see buildings and behaviour; we don't see the values and thought processes that lie beneath. If we want positive change we must rearticulate and affirm the values and challenge the thought processes.

So much of what we do and say is shaped by what lies in the layer of assumptions. These may be defined in part as the ideas and patterns of thought and action that contributed to success in the past – the use of pews, for example. But these may no longer be helpful or likely to lead to success. Once they are out in the open it becomes possible to recognize and challenge outdated or mistaken assumptions and allow the emergence of new attitudes, behaviour and artefacts. This is a more complete way of talking about the habits, assumptions and attitudes referred to earlier as developing over our core identity like a series of geological layers or onion rings.

Culture is notoriously difficult to change. Most agree that it cannot be done if by change we mean *utterly* change. It is impossible to turn a bureaucracy such as a government department into a highly flexible 'adhocracy' such as an advertising agency. The challenge is to help the Church of England be itself, in its own

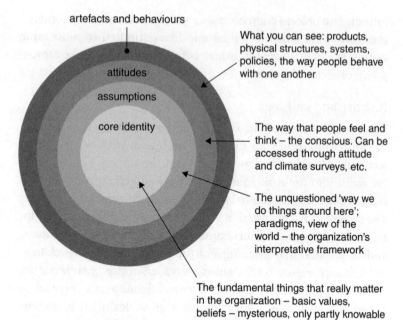

Figure 6.1 Culture onion
Edgar Schein's ideas adapted by Telos Partners Limited

style, but in a healthier and more authentic and effective way – effective, that is, in living out its core purpose and values. Step one is to identify the core; step two is to distinguish the core from the assumptions and 'working practices' that no longer seem valid and are destructive, frustrating the essential purpose. Figure 6.1 posits a model of organizational culture.

Identity in the Church

Does the Church of England, as a religious institution, need to set out its purpose and values? Are they not obvious? Well, no, they are not. In practice there are a host of different answers to the question of purpose and values. One parishioner sees the Church as the guardian of family values, another as a shrine for worship, another as a community of the like-minded, another as an engine of the kingdom. These different views can probably be reconciled but only by placing them in a larger context and by entering a conversation that seeks a genuine enlargement of understanding. This is where we lay the foundations that allow us to define the role of the national Church in today's society – at whatever level the question is being considered. We will not get very far unless we can articulate our self-understanding in terms suited to now. Identity does not change in its essential nature but must be constantly rediscovered and re-expressed in contemporary terms.

Contention in the Church of England

This leads us to another objection and probably the more weighty one, namely that the question of identity is so contended in the Church of England that it cannot be resolved. I addressed this question in Chapter 3 but would like to add some more thoughts here.

In one sense this is a challenge that can only be approached theologically. This does not mean that we need to find a resolution on all the classic areas of theological and ecclesiological disagreement. We do not need clarity or unanimity at that level and will not get it – though it would be useful and fruitful to spend more time in honest and face-to-face discussions of our differences. We do need to get out of our entrenched positions and open our hearts and minds to other perspectives. If we did, we would all be richer.

Nevertheless, the Church of England is and should remain proudly diverse – even if it is currently such that one wonders how diverse an organization can be and yet remain a coherent one.[3] What we should seek is the common ground. We need to ask what we can agree on, what we can all sign up to, and agree to disagree on the rest. It would help if we focused more on practical questions – What is the Church here to do? What are the principles that should guide us on a daily basis? – rather than on technical and higher-order theological debates.

I mentioned in Chapter 3 that when an extremely diverse group of leaders of training institutions met to discuss their purpose and values in these terms, they found sufficient common ground to guide a shared programme and considerable co-operation. When we talk in this fashion our differences seem less significant and our similarities more compelling. It is difficult to say whether this would be possible at the level of the national Church, but is there any reason not to try it? It should certainly be possible at the level of the diocese and parish. There is a risk, of course, of ending up with lowest-common-denominator platitudes – but that is far from inevitable and will depend on the quality of the process and the conversation it allows.

Some may hesitate to open up this discussion on the grounds that it might bring differences that are normally hidden out into the open and be destructive. While this is an understandable concern, the conversation will enrich understanding and enhance a sense of common purpose. This is a prize worth a little discomfort on the way.

Culture in the Church

Do we believe the Church's culture needs to be changed or revitalized? The previous chapter identified some negative features of the Church's culture, notably the lack of rigour, isolation of the clergy and difficulty with difference and conflict. The experience of being part of the Church can be extremely painful. A local church, for example, may continually use the language of family about itself without apparently being aware that families are frequently dysfunctional – the congregation can be destructive as well as a source of comfort and love.

It is obvious that many local churches are alive and well *and* that the Church will always be flawed and fallible. Nevertheless, it is essential to do more. The Church must be a place where new ideas can flourish, faith is related to life as it actually is, community is seen at its best, difference is acknowledged and managed well and truly experienced as the body of Christ. The concern is not only to make the Church a better experience for those already in it. The reality is that the culture of the Church as it is most often experienced will not be attractive to new adherents. And this will not be so much because people outside the Church reject its core purpose and values or its theology but because the Church cannot express these things in a way that has meaning and impact in today's world.

A process for identifying purpose and values

We are talking here about the soul of the organization and of its members. Values are deeply rooted in us and are manifested more emotionally than rationally. In order to identify them we need a process that gets in touch with our feelings so we can examine what lies underneath them. I have found the following process effective – it will probably take two or three separate sessions. This is an activity for the leadership team discussed in the previous chapter.

1 Use photographs or other visual material as a way of accessing people's feelings about the Church, both universal and local. I use a set of photographs depicting human and natural scenes produced by Photolanguage Australia.[4] Set the photos out around the room.

2 Invite the team to look at them all, and ask members to choose one or two each that say something to them about what they value in the Church, both universal and local. Then ask everyone to show the group their photographs and say why they chose them. As people talk, record some of the key words they use on a flip chart.

3 As an alternative or additional activity, invite members of the group to tell stories about times when there was distress or anger in the church and/or about what has caused pleasure and celebration. As they recount stories, ask questions to uncover the value behind the emotional reaction. Someone says, for example, that people get angry when the church is left untidy after an event – it won't take long to discover that some people place a high value on the church as a place of worship, as a sacred space. Again, record the output on a flip chart.

4 Invite the group to consider what they believe to be the reason the church exists – this will require some notion of the purpose of the Church as a whole, but applied to their particular locality or area of concern. Use the words on the flip chart(s) as a prompt. Try to identify the key ideas that emerge and

about which there is agreement. Resist wordsmithing at this stage and resist concern about what outsiders will make of it – this is not a marketing document.

5 This may be as far as you get in a first session. Someone should write up the output and put the material about purpose into draft statement form.

6 The next stage will probably take place at a second session. You might start by considering the draft statement of purpose and agree a final version. This may take time.

7 Take all the words from the first session's 'outputs' that have a values content and reproduce them on cards, one word or phrase per card. If the group contains more than four or five people, divide them into two or three subgroups. Give each group a set of cards and invite them to select their three or four key words or ideas. The groups then share their conclusions – and the reasons for their choices. Allow a discussion about differences and similarities and seek an agreement about the key ideas – do not allow more than about six 'values' as the list needs to be concise to be useful.

8 At the second session also spend time considering the behavioural and 'operational' implications of the purpose and values. What should we stop, start or continue in order to live out our purpose and values? This step is vital if the statements of purpose and value are actually to inform the life of the church.

9 Allow the work done thus far to settle. Someone should take it away and write it up in a more polished fashion. The group should return to it a week or two later to review the work in the light of further thought and reflection.

10 At this stage it may well be revealing to ask: 'If this is what we believe, why does this or that actually happen?' This may help to identify influential mistaken assumptions.

The output of these conversations may look rather bland in the cold light of day. What counts is the conversation – what lies behind the words, and the commitment to what they mean.

Example statements of purpose and values

A Methodist church

Our purpose is to make God's love known in [our locality] – through worship, fellowship and community action.

We seek to interpret the Methodist tradition for the twenty-first century, especially its emphasis on the social gospel. Our values are founded on the recognition that we are all equal in God's eyes and that God is in everyone. They include:

- inclusiveness;
- commitment;
- tolerance and respect;
- spiritual growth;
- community;
- positive change.

An Anglican cathedral

[This] cathedral exists to make real the glory and presence of God in the world.

Our commitment is to:

- live out the teachings of jesus christ in today's world;
- celebrate the presence of god in worship, music and art;
- offer a warm welcome to all who come to the cathedral;
- strengthen church and community life in the diocese;
- challenge injustice at home and abroad;
- promote learning, personal development and spiritual growth.

We value:

- worship;
- hospitality;
- community;
- learning.

Summary of actions

1 Clarify purpose and values using a process like that described above.
2 Expose and challenge assumptions by comparing the espoused or desired with the actual.

3 Develop a positive statement of purpose and values.
4 Be clear what these should now look like in practice – if this is what we believe to be important, what should we continue to do; do more of; do less of? Be particularly rigorous in describing the behaviours that the values imply – this is what will bring the values to life and make the difference.

Time spent getting this right will be time well spent. Clarity about and commitment to shared purpose and values are probably the biggest factors in sustained organizational success.

7

Decide where you want to go

The title for this chapter is another way of talking about vision and strategy, about 'creating the future'. The conversation about identity described in the last chapter had a strongly emotional, personal dimension (see the section 'The task of defining identity'). The conversation about the future is essentially 'rational' – it is about possibilities rather than dreaming dreams. It is still taking place in the team gathered by the leader (see Chapter 5), and the objective is still to produce a hypothesis that can be shared more widely in the next phase of the work.

This chapter begins by describing what is meant by 'vision and strategy' and why it is important to have them. It then addresses objections to planning and concerns about the use of the word 'success'. Finally, it sets out a process for developing a vision and a strategy.

Cameo 8: Questioning assumptions

A group from a parish church was developing a strategy for the next three years. I asked them to describe what they thought would be achieved in three years' time if they were successful. They had some difficulty imagining themselves in the future and describing what was 'now' happening, but after a while they put together a fairly vivid picture.

One of the unexpected benefits of this exercise was that it highlighted some of the group's normally unrecognized assumptions. When we looked at the vision on the flip chart in front of us, a couple of things stood out. First, nearly all their ideas about the future involved more people coming to the church for services or other activities – there was very little about what was happening in the wider community. Second, there

---

was no suggestion that parishioners would be offered any different experiences of worship, such as those usually described now as Fresh Expressions. In this way the church's implicit theology and ecclesiology were revealed and became open to question, which otherwise would probably not have happened.

Vision and strategy

What does the word 'vision' mean to you? A wish list? A divine visitation? An out-of-body experience? A hopeful evocation of something yet to be? None of these are meant here (certainly not a shimmering dream of another world, associated with a deep and unusual spiritual experience); rather, a concrete picture of what will be happening in our world, at a specific time in the medium term, if we are being successful in living out our purpose and values and on the way to realizing our ambition. As noted in the previous chapter, the purpose of NASA is to increase 'man's capability to explore the heavens'. The *vision* was to put a man on the moon by the end of the 1960s.

A vision should be ambitious but realistic; should inspire and guide action. Above all it should offer us a way of judging how successful we are being. It should tell us 'what "good" looks like'.

The term 'strategy' is used in many different ways – sometimes it brings together all the concepts we are using, acting as a way of describing the entirety of the organization's approach and activity. Here the use is more limited and specific: strategy as the initiatives and activities we undertake to move from the current state to the desired future state. The ambition and vision are the ends, the strategy is the means. Both must be consistent with our purpose and values.

A strategy should give us clarity about what we are going to do differently to achieve the desired outcome. This 'difference' is important. Organizations that recognize the need to change their fortunes rarely need a lot more of the same. As suggested in the last chapter, most tend to be stuck in assumptions and habits about what will create success. These may have long ceased to be useful or effective yet we continue to resort to them. I am fond of Einstein's remark that the definition of insanity is 'doing the same thing over and over again and expecting different results'. The strategy needs to offer a convincing account of how we will do different things to get the different result.

Can we plan success?

No doubt some people will be concerned that life cannot be planned, given the uncertain nature of the future, and some will have difficulty with my frequent use of the word 'success'. Let me address both of these.

Concerns about planning

What is the value of this activity when it is obviously true that we cannot control the future and are always at the mercy of events? Is the world not littered with examples of how the 'best-laid schemes o' mice an' men, gang aft agley';[1] how 'life is what happens to you when you are busy making other plans'?

But it is equally true that it is a great deal easier to make decisions about what to do when you know where you are going, and that 'if you don't know where you are going, any road will do'.

A clear picture of the future is both inspiring and enables us to recognize success when we achieve it. It gives us a means of assessing the value of our activity; it enables us to decide what to do *now* – it is an aid to purposeful action. Above all it gives us a real chance of continuing relevance and effectiveness. These things do not happen accidentally. As for the unexpected, when I have a plan I can respond flexibly to new circumstances – I can improvise. Without a plan, I do not know what to do when something comes along – there is no larger frame of reference in which to place the questions the unexpected event poses. In my rock band we find that when we have a clear shape and structure for the song we can add colour and variation successfully. When we do not, and no clarity about what happens when, the thing is simply a mess.

Vision and strategy should not be too tightly defined, so detailed there is no room for the unexpected and the providential. We should always be ready to enjoy the journey, not so driven that we cannot look around us or heed the unexpected tap on the shoulder from the Holy Spirit. But is that really a problem for the Church of England? Are we so focused on creating the future that we cannot live in the present? If we are missing out on life it is more likely to be because we are running round with too little purpose – diaries full of activities whose value we cannot clearly define.

The key is not to be slaves to our vision and strategy and to be prepared to change them as the world changes. They are not an end in themselves, they are a way of enabling us to express what matters to us more relevantly and effectively as the world in which we operate changes. They need to be under regular review – we must treat them as 'living documents'.

The Church and 'success'

The word 'success' is often distrusted in the Church. Some see it as essentially antithetical to the Christian view of the world, which places the 'failure' of the cross at the centre of everything. The Sermon on the Mount tells us that it is the 'unsuccessful' who are blessed. These concerns are understandable. Without question the gospel turns conventional ideas about success upside down; is 'foolishness' to many; has a central narrative of death before resurrection. But this is no reason to reject success or romanticize failure.

First some clarification. Success here means the state of having achieved whatever we set out to achieve – not 'worldly success', such as material rewards, status, self-satisfaction. Nor necessarily having a full church or a rich diocese full of well-attended churches. You can define success however you want. In fact you could define it as heroically hanging on against the odds if that works for you, though that may not appeal to all stakeholders.

My personal take on success is this: Jesus set out to achieve something. He was almost fantastically ambitious – in his proclamation of the kingdom, in the call to make disciples of all the nations. He had a clear view of success – the difference is that his life and teaching profoundly challenges common notions of it. The foolishness of the gospel lies chiefly in this and in his method of achieving success. Jesus' journey to his objective – his 'telos' – involved death and suffering, which is a counter-intuitive way of being successful. But as the letter to the Hebrews says,[2] it was for the joy set before him that Jesus endured the cross – suffering is not embraced *for its own sake* but in the service of a greater purpose. Jesus taught that God wants us to flourish, that the Father gives good things to his children. Note too that Jesus' death resulted from his refusal to compromise on the values and message of the kingdom and that his adherence to them was ultimately vindicated.

Benefits of defining success

I have argued that if we do not define success in the future we do not know what to do in the present – it makes purposeful action a great deal more difficult and we have no way of judging how effective we are or of understanding priorities. Chapter 2 described how much this adds to the stress of the clergy's life – it is to live with a discomfiting voice in our heads asking, 'Am I doing the right thing? Am I doing it well?' If we do not define success in appropriate terms we shall default to the few measures visible to us on a regular basis (the number of 'bums on seats' for example), just as companies that have not asked this question default to defining success in terms of profit.

It sometimes seems as though the language of success is resisted, like the suggestion that it would be useful to have a strategy, precisely because it would reduce the level of ambiguity. If we define what we are trying to achieve we become, in a sense, answerable for it. This is threatening in a culture characterized often by insecurity and a dread of exposure, and may be seen in the anxiety about 'ministerial review', in the inability to give or receive feedback, in the 'us and them' mentality of many clergy towards the diocese. Many would rather endure the stress of a nagging but vague sense of failure than allow themselves to become accountable for something rather more clear-cut. This becomes a vicious circle of avoidance. We need to believe that the truth sets us free and live in the light, and the sooner we do the less painful it will be. It is in the nature of the ministerial task that there will always be ambiguity and that it will always involve doing things to add value in a way that cannot easily be measured. It will always be at least as much about who we are as what we do. But where we can (and we perhaps can more often than we think), let us define success so that we are engaged in purposeful, do-able work, celebrating successes and learning from failures. Let us take blame and the fear of it out of the equation – in short, let us seek a greater maturity in our spiritual lives and in our leadership.

Developing a vision and strategy

It is sometimes helpful to begin by articulating a very high level of ambition. For example, one hospital describes its vision as 'To provide a quality of care we would want for our friends, our families and ourselves.' This is memorable, compelling and engaging. It is lacking in detail but it is vivid and provides a strong base for a more complete vision of success. It sets the standard high and tells everyone immediately that the hospital wants to make a difference in terms that mean something to everyone. Ambition statements of this kind transform the frame of reference, question mindsets and drive action. They get us thinking about potential rather than incremental improvement – the latter is fine, perhaps, in better times than these, but now the Church generally needs more. The ambition may already have been at least partly defined by the leader in initiating the process and setting up the team, but it is important to set it out clearly and ensure it is shared by all.

Key relationships and success

The next step involves the recognition that an organization depends on its relationships – internal and external. If it is to be sustainable it has to be successful in terms that mean something to all parties, not just some. The local church enjoyed by its regular attenders but disliked or distrusted by parishioners has a real problem. The bishop who is a popular and influential figure in wider society but whose ministry is not valued by his clergy has a real problem. Visions of success must take into account all parties' interests and appeal to all key relationships.

A simple way of addressing this is to make a table showing all the key relationships and describe success for 'us' (the organization as a whole) and success for 'them' (the various stakeholder groups both inside and outside it). Ask: 'What constitutes a win for us and a win for the other party?' Consider: 'Can we describe a vision that allows a win for both parties?' The resulting data will provide rich material for the church's vision, and help you develop a basic view of how you define success. Table 7.1

Table 7.1 Success in the context of key relationships

Relationship	Success to us	Success to them
God	God known and named Worked out in learning and living Expressed in and fed by worship 'Seven whole days, not one in seven' Inclusive – 'space for the birds of the trees'	Growing towards adulthood and maturity Understood as working through his whole creation People growing into a more holistic/integrated way of life Present bodies as living sacrifice People in relationship, 'sanctuary' in world
Universal	Being taken seriously (by the media) – as a natural player and a mainstream concern Being perceived as a body of faithfulness and integrity Greater mutuality and interdependence in our overseas links	Being a constant and reliable source of news and comment of quality A resource, for example, prayer, distinctive perspective

87

Relationship	Success to us	Success to them
Internal	Catch the dream Quality of relationships with God and one another Community Liberated, set free To become mature disciples	Clarity Decisive Financially aware With them but not disturbing them Telling what to do
Local church	Active in the local community projects with other bodies Congregations growing in faith and numbers and who reflect their community Increasing numbers involved in leadership and participation	Proactive and interested in what they are doing Helping to make connections and find resources They know we provide high quality and consistent training, for vocations and ministry for example They are confident that we successfully manage our resources, especially financial resources
Community	Mature Christians in the 'marketplace' – listening, interpretative Ambassadors for Christ Trying to stand in others' shoes – experiencing their reality, their needs Mutual respect Voice in times of change	Seen as a community ourselves Help with meaning, identity Confident in ourselves Language that communities can understand

offers an example of success in the context of key relationships – the 'win/win' – as described by one bishop's staff team.

Scanning the horizon

I suggested in Chapter 2 that creating the future is about understanding what is happening in the environment in which you operate, about understanding what you will need to do to be relevant in the changing world. It is vital, therefore, that the leadership team gives some time to scanning the horizon and understanding what is going on. This is likely to involve some research. At the local church level it will mean, for example, understanding the changes that are taking place in the local community – in demographics, local policy, planning and so forth. How will we change to meet these new challenges and opportunities? If we become aware that the parish is likely to contain many more families with young children, for example, it is likely to influence our choices about our pattern of services and weekly activities.

It is important to be aware of larger trends too, even if prediction is notoriously difficult and caution is advised about any particular conclusion. Here are some of the ways the world served by the Church of England is changing:

- The proportion of older people is increasing : 19.2 per cent of the population will be over 65 by 2021.[3]
- Internet-based social networking is a still-growing phenomenon – might it become a serious alternative to face-to-face meeting?
- Traditional authorities have to make their case along with everyone else – they cannot assume influence or respect.
- There are few agreed 'public meanings' – everyone has to invent their own meaning.
- The need to protect the natural environment is an increasing priority.
- The young generation knows next to nothing about the Christian faith.
- There is likely to be an increasingly significant role for voluntary organizations in the provision of community services.

Some of these trends are not particularly new but the Church has not been notably energetic or deliberate in addressing them. It is not a matter, either, of simply going along with them by, for example, creating 'virtual church' – though that may have a part to play. It might rather be a matter of underlining the role of the Church as a rare source of real community, as an even rarer source of what someone called 'serious space' – a place where a serious conversation can be held. For where else is there?

These enquiries can be given shape by making use of tools such as a 'SWOT' or 'PESTLE' analysis. SWOT involves looking at internal factors (Strengths and Weaknesses) and external factors (Opportunities and Threats). The key with a SWOT analysis is not just to make a list but to relate one part to another. You use it to analyse how the strengths can be used and weaknesses mitigated in addressing opportunities and threats. PESTLE is a tool – a checklist if you like – for ensuring you address all the external factors, and involves looking at Political, Economic, Sociological, Technological, Legal and Environmental changes that may have an impact on the future of the organization.

Clearly the depth and sophistication of the research and analysis required will vary according to the scale and complexity of the organization concerned. One would expect it to be a simpler exercise for the parish than the diocese.

Considering potential

Most planning about the future tends to start with what we believe we are currently capable of, and proposes incremental improvements year on year. It can be much more exciting and productive to consider what we might have the potential to do or be. We might, for example, look at what others are doing. If another church can do this or that a great deal better than us, could we not perhaps do it too by learning from them and perhaps radically changing our approach? Or we can look at our resources and environment differently. Let us imagine a church that wishes to maintain its contact with its parishioners but now has too few members to deliver the parish magazine to everyone. What if it devoted the same resources to a website that was kept up to date instead? Someone says, 'But not everyone has access to the internet.' Is that true? Might finding out be an opportunity to engage with the parish? Might there be other ways of keeping those who do not have internet access up to date?

Or at the diocesan level we might assume that a drive to encourage mission in the parishes might be hampered by the limited extent to which the bishop can influence them, depending as he does on working through a staff team and other intermediaries. One diocese has questioned the assumption that the layers have to operate in the conventional way, and has organized its deaneries as missionary units with area deans designated as missioners reporting directly to the bishop. This is not to suggest that this is the 'right answer' or that it would work everywhere. The point of this activity is to unearth and challenge assumptions that limit us and prevent us from reaching our full potential – to think differently.

Building the vision

All the data gathered as a result of the work done to date should be used to generate a vision of the desired future. The statement of vision should be as concrete, vivid and specific as possible – it is describing the outcome rather than the intention. Imagine yourselves two, three or four years ahead describing what is actually happening. For example:

- 'The proportion of 25–30-year-olds in our congregation is now 50 per cent higher' (parish).
- 'Some 75 per cent of parishes are offering opportunities for enquirers' (diocese).
- 'The Church of England is being recognized in the media for its innovative approach to reaching out to its communities' (national).

In a diocese the vision needs to embrace parish life and aim to create a direction and picture of future success into which most or all will be able to buy. But it will probably be best to leave plenty of space for individual parishes to describe the vision and pursue it in terms that make sense to them and their churchmanship, and space to shape their own lives without undue interference. The whole enterprise should create clarity about what we do and commit to together, as a diocese, and what we leave to the wisdom of the individual parishes.

It is helpful to break the vision down into four distinct areas – this both focuses thinking and ensures all the key subjects are covered (see Table 7.2). The questions under the headings in each box are by way of example and are far from a complete list of what should be taken into consideration.

Table 7.2 A framework for developing a vision statement

Our relationships internally	*Our relationships externally*
How are we organized?	How do we work with the wider
What is it like being part	population?
of our community?	How do we relate to the external world?
	How do we relate to the larger Anglican
	Church?
Size and scope	*Facilities and infrastructure*
How big are we?	What buildings and other physical
What income do we have?	resources do we have?
What 'services' do we provide?	How are we using our infrastructure?

Here is a process for carrying out this task. Put a piece of flip-chart paper on the wall for each of the four headings. Each member of the team takes a number of post-it notes and writes a description of *one* aspect of the future on each. Everyone then puts their post-its under the appropriate heading on the flip-chart paper. The group then gathers round the flip charts, organizing the post-its into themes and subject areas. Someone then takes the charts away and writes them up and perhaps also produces a draft or 'straw man' version with some provisional choices in the areas where ideas differed in the initial exercise. The group receives both the unexpurgated 'outputs' and the straw man. When the group next meets they consider both and agree on a 'final' version. 'Final' is in quotation marks because we are still talking about a hypothesis rather than the finished product. The final form of the vision may depart from the format, but it is a useful starting point.

Strategy

Once the vision is agreed, the next step is to develop a strategy for achieving it, 'strategy' denoting the principal means by which we will get from 'here' to 'there'. But we cannot do that without understanding better where 'here' is. We have to ask questions like, 'How well are we doing now? What resources do we have?' and so forth. Some might wonder whether we should consider these questions before getting too ambitious about the future. It is quite likely, of course, that the whole process has been prompted by a recognition that something has to be done to address a pressing problem. But aside from recognizing that, I have not encouraged beginning with a full exploration of the status quo. Might we get a more realistic outcome if we did? The problem is that taking the process that way round has a tendency to condition conversations about the future negatively and trap us in the less helpful mindsets of the present. It is better to think fresh and challenge assumptions if the aim is to do something different – we will not solve tomorrow's problems with the assumptions we brought to yesterday's.

But the less optimistic will be pleased to hear that there is now a necessity to take a look at what Jim Collins calls the 'brutal reality'.[4] This involves describing the present as honestly as possible, which may be difficult in an institution that prizes consensus and dislikes conflict. Individuals may need to hear some difficult messages and some cherished illusions may need to be shattered. This needs to be handled with care and as objectively and positively as possible, but nothing will be gained by pretending things are better than they are. Here are some extracts from how one public sector body described its brutal reality:

- lack of known/agreed approaches to key business issues;
- lack of thinking space;
- weakness in management skills/capacity;
- lack of disciplined working;
- lack of financial viability;
- need a greater focus to basic care delivery;
- ineffectual management;
- lack of strategic board leadership;
- lack of individual top-team ownership;
- 'won't change' culture;
- lack of clear management objectives/agenda;
- poor at translating ideas into action (detail).

It might be that the brutal reality cannot be described by the group working together – it may be too difficult to be honest. If that is the case, it might be helpful to have a neutral party interview each of the leadership team members ahead of the group process to allow views to be expressed privately and presented back to the group in consolidated, organized and anonymous fashion. This still requires the group to engage in an honest exchange about the material presented. Is it how things really are? Do we all agree?

It is, of course, equally important to recognize and celebrate the successes and the positive foundations for future growth. But if there is to be sustainable change there will need to be some real dissatisfaction with the present. No one works hard to fix something they do not really believe is broken. Frequently the leadership team is more aware of the 'burning platform' than the rest of the organization (though the other way round is not unknown!), and it will be necessary to describe it clearly in the next phase of the process.

After this discussion, the leadership team should move next to setting out the principal actions and initiatives it is proposing to address the reality and realize the vision. It is also very helpful to be able to identify very clear first steps and, if possible, some 'quick wins'; that is, a few positive changes that can be made more or less immediately – this builds confidence in the process. If the group has done the work to date well, the strategic initiatives should 'fall out' pretty easily. At this stage there is no value in developing these into a full-scale business plan – you have enough to take the discussion to the rest of the organization.

On a practical note, some of the discussion required in this stage can be run parallel to discussions described in the previous chapter. The two or three meetings recommended for the identity work can also at least begin the development of vision and strategy.

Summary of actions

1 Clarify and articulate ambition.
2 Describe success in terms of your key relationships.
3 Research trends and other environmental factors.
4 Describe your vision for the medium-term future.
5 Develop a strategy – probably a small number of principal actions/initiatives – to achieve it, built on an honest assessment of the 'brutal reality', but also the organization's potential.

Here is an example of how one Regional Training Partnership (RTP) captured its vision and its strategy. Note that the latter is at this stage expressed as 'first steps' rather than a complete strategy – this is a work in progress.

Regional Training Partnership vision statement
Our vision for 2010

- The benefits of partnership being realized and recognized within and beyond the region;
- The RTP seen as the exemplar of an effective RTP;
- A 'learning pathway' clearly in place across the region;
- The number of people participating in training across the region up by 10 per cent;
- Costs per head of people training across the region down by 10 per cent;
- Provision to 'train the trainer' in place;
- A regional solution for discipleship education in place;
- Initial Ministerial Education (IME) years 1–7 far more integrated;
- More consistent, appropriate and comprehensive;
- Continuing Ministerial Education (CME) in place;
- Greater integration of authorized lay ministry training;
- Web-based learning schemes being planned;
- The partnership governance and structure established;
- Real trust between partners developing;
- The RTP operating as a powerful voice for trainers and users in the region.

Our first steps (the year to May 2007)

Reconstitute the steering group: to include more trainers (probably a representative from the principal 'first-steps' groups).
   The steering group to:

- Lead on producing a covenant, or declaration of intent to, on which the regional partnership will be based;
- Provide oversight for the 'first-steps' groups;
- Develop a job description and recruiting process for a coordinator.

First-steps groups to meet and address:

- education for discipleship;
- IME 1–7;
- CME;
- authorized lay ministry.

And perhaps:

- train the trainer;
- Fresh Expressions;
- website.

And also:

- Each first-steps group to create 'terms of reference' for their work and where new funding is required, and a business case – then take appropriate action.
- Each of the main first-steps groups to include one of the region's church leaders.
- Partners to ensure their strategic thinking is shared with other partners.
- Hold conference May 2007 to review progress.

8

Get everyone involved

All the work you have done to date still has the status of a hypothesis. It is well considered, a framework to guide action, but not complete – there will probably still be some questions, some parts of the picture to be filled in. It is better if there is still something for others to do. Your people will know that you have been thinking about the future of the Church (at whatever level you lead), you may have gathered data from them that has informed your thinking, but the discussion has remained within the leadership team. Now it is time to share it with them.

This chapter describes what is meant by engaging others and considers some issues that may arise, such as whether the process is too top-down or, conversely, too bottom-up. It sets out a process for engaging key audiences and provides some advice on managing the meetings involved.

Cameo 9: Excited and energized

The Roman Catholic Sisters held two rounds of meetings in every one of their five regions, attended by Sisters and, latterly, staff to give them a say in the development of the new vision and strategy. This added up to well over 100 meetings in about 18 months, every one of which was attended by the Superior General. She explained the leadership's thinking and sat with the participants at each workshop as they developed their response. This represented an immense commitment, particularly as the regions include the United States, South Africa and Australia. What was noticeable was the extent to which the participants became excited and energized at the meetings about the possibilities of the future. Sisters spoke passionately about what mattered to them. Several described the process as spiritually reinvigorating. There is no doubt that it would have been very difficult to make the changes necessary in the organization without these meetings, and that it was the presence of the Superior General that was key to both reassuring and inspiring the Sisters.

The task of engagement

I described earlier the response I got when my decision to exclude the donkey from the Palm Sunday service became known – for most, this was only as we gathered in the car park for the procession into church. This was a relatively small matter, but how do you feel when someone announces a change about which you have been neither informed nor consulted? Unless it is very minor or does not really concern you, your reaction might be negative. It might also make you less inclined to get involved, less co-operative.

If you want your strategy to have any real effect, people need to receive it and support it. To make that more likely, you need to invite them to help shape it – we support what we have been consulted about, what we feel heard on. But it is not only a matter of support. 'Employee engagement' is a popular subject now. The engaged employee makes 'discretionary energy' available; that is, gives more than compliance. There is a growing recognition that the most effective organizations cannot manage everything from the top. Leaders need to work with people who feel willing and able to exercise initiative and make things happen themselves. People in organizations can do this if they understand the strategy – that is, have a framework to guide useful action – and feel engaged to the point where they want to act. Furthermore, the membership of any organization is a huge source of knowledge and expertise. If this is acknowledged and used, people feel more engaged. But at the same time the organization benefits in that it is likely to make better plans – for there will be many people with insights not available to the leadership team.

Two features of the Church of England make the process of engagement vital. Its leadership is carried out in a highly distributed fashion, largely by people who are independent. It is also highly dependent on the work of volunteers who do not face financial consequences if members of the congregation vote with their feet. When you add to the mix the lack of any great culture of obedience, it is evident that it is virtually impossible to make anybody in the Church of England do something they do not want to do. They have to believe in what is being proposed.

Engagement and mobilization

The task, then, is not simply to share information with others or even to consult them but to *engage* them. You are inviting members of the organization to hear what you have concluded but also to enter into something like the process that you have been through. The aim is to take people 'on the journey', to enter into the issues, to help shape the conclusions and 'own' them for themselves. In addition, people will be invited to consider the implications of the purpose, values, vision and strategy for them, in their roles – both to tell you what this will mean in practice and to prepare for action themselves. Part of the purpose is to *mobilize* people – you are making them partners in the creation of the future.

Leadership involvement

The fact that leadership should not seek to control the discussion too closely does not mean it should not be involved. The engagement phase should involve everyone in the organization. The leadership team cannot conduct this phase on its own but it cannot simply leave it to others. Its direct involvement conveys messages about the importance of the process and the value placed on the input of people at large, which influences the perception of authenticity and builds a sense of real partnership. If the leaders are committed, so are the people more likely to be. If the organization is to change then the leaders had better be in the forefront modelling the changed approach. Far too many leaders think that everyone else has to change but not them. The change needs to start with leaders.

The right approach?

Too top-down?

Why present a 'straw man'? Why condition the conversation in this way? Why not invite those at the 'front line' to make their own suggestions, based on their grassroots experience and knowledge?

The process proposed here is preferable to starting with a blank page because when you do that, the result tends to be confusion rather than a productive conversation. It is too big a task, especially with a large group. Of course you want to hear what those with expertise and experience have to say, but it is better to invite them to react to something – freely – than to start from scratch. And as said above, leaders need to lead – initiate and frame the process, put something considered on the table. This is an appropriate and practical approach – most people will also expect it and be concerned if leaders seem unwilling to lead.

Having said all that, there is no reason why a range of people should not be invited to offer their views as individuals or in focus groups at an earlier stage of the process to inform the leadership team's deliberations.

Too open?

On the other hand, the openness implied in the above process troubles many leaders. I distinctly remember a senior manager in a police force saying, 'How can we discuss this with anyone until we have all the answers?' The assumption here is that it is leadership's job to answer all the questions, which is one that plagues many organizations. It creates an unnecessary burden for leaders, fails to harness all the skills, knowledge and expertise available and inhibits the development of an organization's people. The role of the leader is to create the environment, initiate the building of the strategic framework, to hold people to the task – to manage and lead the *process* rather than to know everything.

The parallel anxiety is that this process will open up a dangerously free discussion that might go 'the wrong way'. In other words, the people might have a very different view from the leadership. Chaos and confusion will be the outcome. Well, if there really is such a big difference in perspective between leadership and people, then it had better be brought into the open and addressed if the organization is not to be mired in internal tension and wrangling (even if it only takes a passive-aggressive form). In fact it does not happen as leaders fear. If the leadership goes about its task honestly and carefully it will probably arrive at a view of the organization that is substantially shared by its people. If it says to people, 'This is how it looks to us; how does it look to you?' people will add to the picture, amend some details but share the basic analysis. If it says – even if it is not put quite thus – 'Here is the new strategy, take it or leave it', then you can be sure people will find fault with most of it and resist its implementation. This is partly a matter of psychology – people respond better to what is placed before them as a possibility rather than as a fait accompli. But it is also about the mindset in which leaders do their thinking; about what informs the material, what attitudes have shaped what is brought to people, the fact that it is a *hypothesis*. Is this a search for truth or an imposition of personal views? The former gets much better results. Perhaps this will be obvious in an organization like the Church of England whose values, structure, independence of its officers and dependence on volunteers make the engagement option the only viable choice.

The process of engagement

Key audiences and the order of play

The engagement process starts with the identification of the key audiences. In a parish, the obvious groups would be the PCC and the congregation. If the congregation is large, it may need to be divided up in some way. The wider parish probably cannot and probably should not be included at this stage. Although there is a real sense in which every parishioner is a member of the local church, it is neither practical nor necessary to involve them in the engagement activity proper. There will be value in communicating its outcome at a later stage. In a diocese the picture is far more complex. Key audiences will include: diocesan staff; clergy and accredited ministers; congregations plus the synodical structure (bishop's council, diocesan and deanery synods). It may be right to include ecumenical partners. The leadership team will need a strategy to reach all these groups.

In a parish, unless the numbers are very large the leadership team can probably handle the work itself. The PCC is the right place to start because formally speaking it has, with the incumbent, the responsibility and authority for parish life. The congregation can be reached in a meeting, or meetings, depending on numbers.

In a diocese there are options, but it could look like this, in roughly chronological order:

1 Engage the bishop's council first – this is a senior group whose support and input is essential.
2 Create a 'conduit group' of people who will help the leadership team engage others. The obvious candidates would be a mixture of rural or area deans and diocesan officers, led by a member of the leadership team, such as a suffragan bishop. If such a group is chosen, they will need to be themselves engaged; that is, given an opportunity to consider and contribute to the hypothesis produced by the leadership team first and given the support and training necessary to manage the rest. The role of the group is to make the process happen – its members will support it by leading meetings and will need the administrative support to make all the arrangements required.
3 Hold a meeting or meetings for diocesan staff.
4 Use the deanery or archdeaconry structures – depending on numbers – to hold meetings for clergy. As those who share the bishop's ministry, it seems right to engage them as a specific group.
5 At the same time a series of meetings aimed at congregations should be set up. This could be managed through special meetings of the deanery synods or by special meetings in each benefice if this is practical. Clergy should be invited to these as well, of course, if only to avoid any suggestion that the process is intended to get at the laity and by-pass the clergy.

6 Devote a whole diocesan synod to the same task. Since many, if not all, members will have been engaged through other channels, the character of the meeting could be more of a reflection by the leadership on what it has heard and the conclusions it has drawn, with further feedback from the synod. This will need to be judged according to how the engagement timetable works out.

This looks, and is, a formidable undertaking, especially as it will be far better if a member of the leadership team is present at, and contributes to, every meeting. The impact of it will be transformative, however, and it is worth the effort. It is better to move more slowly than one would like and cover the ground properly than rush it and skimp. Having said that, momentum is an important factor in successful organizational change, so there should be no unnecessary delays, and good, frequent communication about progress. It is vital there be no perception that the process is disappearing into the long grass or that it is all talk with no consequence or follow-up. This is not an activity that can be fitted in alongside a whole lot of other initiatives – these should be placed on one side for the duration of the process, and business as usual kept to a minimum. The aim is to create the future for the diocese, to ensure it is successful (in whatever terms you decide) for the next ten years (at least). It should be the absolute priority call on people's time.

The meetings

An engagement meeting can be run in 'conference' style – it is possible to run one for 50–100 people at a time. It needs to give participants enough time to go on a journey like that undertaken by the leadership, which argues for a day or at least a half-day meeting. Engagement meetings are better facilitated by someone other than the incumbent or bishop – this allows the leaders to contribute without having to worry about managing the whole meeting. In the diocese this is probably a member of the conduit group. In either case it could be an external consultant. Agendas should include the following:

1 Introduction by facilitator – why we are here, what we plan to achieve and so forth.
2 Background and context – in the parish this should be delivered by the incumbent, in the diocese by a member of the leadership team, ideally the diocesan bishop himself. This should explain what the process is all about – why we're doing it, what we hope to achieve, the principles on which it has been based. This will include some account of the 'brutal reality', the challenge or problem clearly stated. The address must set the scene, ideally be inspirational and if necessary sobering – it is vital people understand that there is something at stake here.
3 The group should be given a chance to discuss and respond to this presentation. They could be asked to consider 'what they liked', 'what concerned them' and 'what they would add'. This should be done in small groups followed by plenary.
4 The facilitator should set out the activity to date and to follow in process terms.
5 The leadership team's hypothesis for creating the future should then be set out in such a way that it can be considered in manageable chunks and a full response made.
6 The responses should be heard and recorded.
7 Some kind of summary should be attempted by those leading the meeting, and the next steps clearly described.

In either dioceses or parishes, the numbers likely to be gathered for most of the meetings will be large – the consideration of the leadership's straw man will need to be undertaken in smaller groups, followed by plenary discussion. A method we have found invaluable over the years is to present the hypothesis in the form of a worksheet. The purpose, values and vision are set out with questions inviting the participants to score and amend what is presented and also, critically, consider the implications of what is being proposed, for the diocese or parish and for them. This is a large document – printed on A0 paper (c.84 × 119 cm) and laminated so that a group of six or so can gather round it and work together and record their thoughts easily. We normally only allow one pen per group – the special marker pen for laminated surfaces – so that the group has to debate and agree before insert-ing its responses! The facilitator can manage this in different ways. He or she can brief the groups so that they complete the whole worksheet in one go or so that they do it in chunks, gathering feedback in plenary from the groups on that section before they move on to the next. In plenary sessions each group should be invited to feed back the highlights of their discussion – not every-thing they wrote on the worksheet. The worksheets can be stuck on the walls so that everyone can read the full responses. The content of the worksheets should be recorded after the meeting and distributed to all participants. This is an onerous task for the secretariat but it is very important to reassure participants that they have indeed been heard. If worksheets are not used, then whatever has been recorded on flip charts or other media should be likewise recorded and distributed. If resources make preprinted, laminated worksheets impractical, the same principles can be applied using smaller and more cheaply produced 'work books'.

Follow up

Whatever is said at these meetings should be recorded, key mes-sages identified and the resulting document copied and made available to all. These messages will need to be presented back to the leadership team, who will have to decide what amendments to make to the strategy document in the light of what they have heard – this will be a matter of judgement. Those engaged can influence the outcome but that does not mean everyone gets what they want. The amended version of the strategy can then be formally re-presented to the parish via the PCC and, perhaps, annual meeting, or to the diocese through the synodical system, for approval and decision.

Handling negativity

It is probable that leaders will encounter negativity and cynicism at some point in the process, though it is likely to be a bigger factor in dioceses than parishes. It may well be most evident in the clergy, who are more prone to see diocesan initiatives as 'interference'. This is one reason why it may be better to address clergy in separate meetings. Bishops and their teams may well hear people say that the process will come to nothing, that it will make no difference, that it is a waste of time and money, that it is an unwarranted interference, that it represents a lack of trust in clergy and parishes, or that they have sold out to the management consultants. It is important to listen to these views, even if some take the form of a rant. Wherever negative views are expressed, leaders should avoid defending themselves and instead seek to listen and understand. When they have listened fully, they also need to articulate clearly their determination to see the process through and create a better future for the parish or diocese. Bishops also need to be clear that the intention is to create a framework for the diocese that will leave a great deal of room for individual parishes to express themselves in a way consistent with their churchmanship. Micro-management is not on the agenda. Some individuals may need further conversations 'offline' rather than take up too much time in the meeting.

There will probably also be objections in the diocese from those who believe that their theologies differ too greatly from their colleagues' or their bishop's to make the conversation productive or a useful outcome likely. Again, it is right to listen, not to defend, but to invite those who believe this to test the process and find out what can or cannot be achieved through it.

It is vital not to be thrown off course by these reactions. In the end most will be won over by a combination of listening, genuine engagement and the sheer persistence that demonstrates that the bishop means business. Some will not, but in any change process there will be some who cannot or will not play. They should not be allowed to subvert or stall the process and need to be kindly but firmly side-lined. If they will not join in, let them go.

Summary of actions

1 Identify the key audiences.
2 Determine a strategy for reaching each of them.
3 If necessary, constitute, engage and train a conduit group.
4 Plan the engagement meetings.

5 Design and produce any materials required.
6 Hold the meetings.
7 Ensure that all 'outputs' are recorded, consolidated and made available to the participants.
8 Amend and finalize your statements about purpose, values, vision and strategy.

9

Make it happen

At this point you have an agreed strategy that is widely 'owned' and supported. In a diocese it might have taken 12 to 18 months to get to this point. Now the hard work begins. You have reached the point where the talking stops and planning and action is required – you are entering the change process 'proper'.

This chapter explores some of the ways people respond to change and suggests approaches to managing it. It considers some of the difficulties the Church might face in making and implementing ambitious plans. Finally, it describes the planning process and suggests some critical success factors.

Cameo 10: Change becomes a reality

Two of the Roman Catholic Congregation's regions decided to improve their computer systems as one of the first objectives in their regional plans. They wanted to introduce software that would bring together all their care management and business data and enable greater efficiency and easier access to important information. It would, for example, allow everything to be 'inputted' once, make it easier to keep accurate records about residents and automate functions such as calculations of salary payments for staff.

This was quite an undertaking for an organization unused to concerted action and large programmes. The project had a number of stages. In the first place the regions had to audit and then upgrade all their computers, networks, broadband connections and basic software. This process produced some tensions. It exposed people to a hitherto unknown level of scrutiny and revealed some rather poor existing practice. It brought 'demanding' strangers into the houses, whose presence was often seen as disruptive. There were many problems of communication,

---

with faults on both sides. With the benefit of hindsight it is now clear that some aspects of the project could have been managed better. There were many faults reported in the new systems in the early days: sometimes breakdowns that turned out to be the result of Sisters taking plugs out unaware of the consequences; sometimes problems that resulted from inadequate specification in the planning stage. The new hardware and software brought with it new protocols that were quite antithetical to the informal style that had been characteristic of the houses.

Then the new care management software itself had to be installed and people taught how to use it. Many of the houses welcomed it as a way of making their work easier and more efficient. Some were less enthusiastic. Some Sisters and staff did not want to change their old systems, many of them paper-based or even handwritten. Some staff realized that they would be paid for the hours they actually worked and, rightly, did not think this would work in their favour. Many saw the whole thing as an imposition from the centre, bringing with it a loss of discretion and control.

Now the new system is bedded in, most could not imagine going back to the old ways. Houses are more in control of their operation, their work is easier, residents benefit from a more consistent service and costs are reduced. The regions as a whole are benefitting as work is carried out to consistent standards across the houses, and they enjoy greater access to all the important information about how the houses are doing.

All in all, the IT project brought home the reality of change in a way that all the talking had not!

Managing change

In this phase what has been discussed as an idea becomes a reality. It is at this point that enthusiasm can be lost and resistance become apparent.

Responses to change

It will be important to be aware of how people react to change. They may support it conceptually, but their emotional reaction in the face of the reality may well be different.

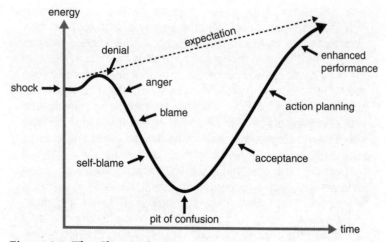

Figure 9.1 The Change Curve

Based on research in Elisabeth Kübler-Ross, *On Death and Dying* (London: Routledge, 1969)

The Change Curve model (see Figure 9.1) is based on Dr Elisabeth Kübler-Ross's research into how individuals react to bereavement and will be familiar territory to those with experience of pastoral ministry. The emotional journey it describes is experienced by those undergoing virtually any kind of shock or change – a fact that underlines the point that the emotional reaction to change is frequently one of grief. Robert Hockley, an Australian change-consultant and academic, remarks that 'Change = Loss + Gain'.[1] The process we have been exploring in this book is designed to maximize the sense of 'gain' but the loss part of the equation cannot and should not be ignored.

It is quite common for people leading change to imagine that everyone will react to the changes with the enthusiasm they them-selves feel for them. They tend to forget that they have already had time to deal with their emotional reactions – and may have forgotten that they had them. The fact that they are leading the change and consequently feel as though they have some control over what is happening lends a sense of security not so readily available to others. This also emphasizes how important the engagement process is – it should give more people precisely this sense of control and ownership.

It is easy to be misled by an initially positive reaction, just as one can be when bereavement is characterized in the early stages by a burst of energy, even an odd euphoria ('Isn't he/she brave?'). This is because the first stage in the process is denial – an inability to take in what is happening. Soon enough people head off down the emotional slope. What follows could be seen as a succession of strategies for dealing with the situation, none of which can work but which allow the individual to avoid the reality of the situation. Another way of looking at it is to see it as a series of emotional reactions that have a kind of logic. At any rate, there is a typical pattern. Those presented with change become angry with others – with you, the instigator of change, perhaps. They then look for others to blame – again, perhaps you, the instigator of change – it is your fault all this is happening to me. The next step is self-blame – it's my fault; I cannot cope; I'm not up to this; I've failed. These reactions spent and the world unchanged by them, the exhausted individual plunges into the pit of confusion, unable to know what to think or feel. In time people come up from the pit and accept the new reality – an acceptance that allows them to plan how they will work with it and to begin to operate within the new world.

This emotional journey will be made by everyone confronted with change. For some the curve will be relatively shallow and the timescale shorter. Others will plunge deep and take a long time to emerge. Sometimes people get stuck somewhere on the down slope – they may become functional but emotionally they are still there. These variations will be factors of how significant the change is, how emotionally robust individuals are and what else is going on in their lives.

Leading change

There are a number of important implications for people leading change. First, the less of a shock the change is, the better – the more people are prepared and have helped to create the change, the more likely they will deal with it relatively easily. Second, the process is inevitable – the leader must understand this and not be surprised by it. Third, the leader cannot 'solve' it – no amount of explanation or cajoling will help. What then can he or she do?

Put simply, the only helpful strategy is to listen and understand. This may be challenging as it is likely to involve resisting the temptation to react to anger with anger or defensive explanations. The only useful thing to do is to listen to what people have to say, help them to say it. It is not about sympathizing but about acknowledging the emotional reality. This will help individuals move on, but only they can take the steps. The team leading change will do well to cultivate its listening skills. Of course, everything I've described is well understood in the Church and regularly practised in its pastoral role. That does not mean it is always so well practised in its internal life – physician, heal thyself! The skills are almost certainly already there – it will be a matter of applying them.

When confronted with a proposal for change, people will typically divide into three categories (see Figure 9.2).

There will be a small number of enthusiasts ('advocates'). You will be grateful for their help and energy but they can be offputting for people in the other two categories. The largest group is those who are concerned but take a fairly logical approach. They are sceptical but willing to be convinced. The final, and again

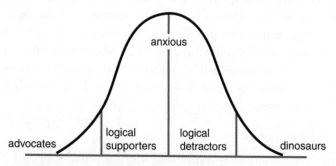

- Advocates need no convincing
- Logical *anxious* people will decide whether to give their support based on how things align with their purpose, vision and values
- 'Dinosaurs' will not change – they may comply

Figure 9.2 Change distribution curve

Used by Telos Partners Limited

much smaller group, the 'dinosaurs' or 'refuseniks', will never accept the change. This latter category may also include people like the leader I met who knew the change had to happen but also knew he could not be part of it. It is terribly tempting to put all your energy into trying to win round people in this group but it is a mistake to do so – nothing you do will succeed. The only realistic strategy is to manage them so that they are not able to derail the change process. This will mean redeployment, perhaps, or simply acting to minimize the damage they can do in roles they will not leave – both need to be done as honestly and kindly as possible. If a change is happening and there are some people who can neither stop nor live with it, the best thing for all is probably for them to move on. Some will see it that way, others will not! Do not indulge those determined to be martyrs with too much attention.

The group that should have most attention is the large group of anxious but reasonable people. They will further divide into those disposed to accept and those disposed to reject the change. The best strategy is to make the case as strongly as you can and help the logical supporters win over the logical detractors.

All this assumes that the change you propose is well thought through, logical, consistent with the organization's understanding of itself and the available data on the environment, and that every effort has been made to engage the organization in shaping it. If any of these factors is missing then do not be surprised if the case proves hard to make. You will also have sacrificed the legitimacy you need for dealing with the refuseniks. On the other hand, if you have been through the process described in this book and done it with integrity, then you have the right at this stage to assert that the time for discussion is over, the decision made, and insist on action.

The demand for focused action

Some of this the Church will do well, particularly the sympathetic treatment of people facing change. Other aspects of change management may come less easily.

Does the Church possess the capacity for change?

One of the problems many organizations face is that as the need for change becomes more urgent, the capacity for change diminishes. Typically, as organizations get into difficulties they respond by reducing costs, which means reducing capacity – there is less money and fewer people available. The dioceses facing the greatest difficulties are the most likely to lack people with specialist skills and leadership with the necessary time and experience.

This means that if the Church of England is to change while it still has a measure of control over the change, it needs to do it soon. The paradox here is that change is more readily accepted when it is evident to everyone that the current ways of working are broken or ineffective, but that point often comes too late. It is better to change while you still can.

And the capacity issue makes it all the more important that change not be attempted half-heartedly or without proper focus of energy or resources. If it is to make a real difference, change programmes need to be given clear priority.

Is there a willingness to take action and follow through?

There are two possible issues here. One is that any process of change will involve some conflict – at some point, not everyone will like what is happening and leadership will be tempted to back off rather than follow through. This is particularly likely to happen in the Church because the culture finds dealing with conflict so inimical.

The second issue is that successful change requires a willingness to keep at it and work out the details well past the point at which the process is particularly interesting or exciting in itself. In my experience the gritty process of implementation is less attractive to clergy than the earlier, more conceptual stages.

There is no simple answer to this, other than the commitment to see it through, perhaps allied to a determination to make use of the skills of those for whom implementation is more congenial. But in the latter case, the leadership cannot afford to 'move on' to more interesting things while the process remains uncompleted.

The reality will probably be messy at times – there will be hiccups and misunderstandings, and perhaps above all, determination and persistence are required. If you do stick at it you will be amazed at the strides you take. Look back and see how far you have come and let that encourage you to keep going. I have spoken of creating the future. Of course we cannot truly do that, but faith does not stand around hoping either that God will sort it all out or that, against all the evidence, what worked in the past will work in the future. Faith recognizes that change is built into the gospel and embraces it intelligently. In short, we must do what we can and trust God for the rest.

Planning

A 'change team'?

Early consideration should be given to how you plan to steer the overall implementation process. One of the biggest challenges is combining all the regular activity – what companies call 'business as usual' – with introducing new ways of working and/or new activities. You will need to decide if the implementation of the new strategy can be managed from within the existing structures – the parish or diocesan staff teams – or whether the scope and ambition of the new strategy require a 'change team' to focus on creating the new world while others deal with business as usual. The decision will most likely rest on the scale of the changes envisaged. The implementation could quite properly be led by the team – the conduit group discussed in Chapter 8 – who managed the engagement process, though consideration should be given to whether changes may be required to reflect the need for different knowledge and skills.

Launching the strategy

You may wish to signal the beginning of the implementation phase by holding some form of 'strategy launch' in the form, perhaps, of a day conference. This is a more practical proposition for a parish or a church organization but a diocese could have, for example, a special meeting of the diocesan synod with other invitees. This step is not essential but it is useful as a means of celebrating the work to date, presenting the completed work and signalling and starting the implementation phase. It also demonstrates an intention to keep people involved in influencing and shaping what happens. The event would describe the implementation process, clarify the role of the leadership, its expectations of others, the support to be offered and, ideally, describe some early changes – 'quick wins' that will encourage people and demonstrate you all mean business.

The planning process

The first big practical step is to translate what might well be still a fairly high-level strategy into more complete plans. In the diocese this will probably involve inviting key groups – such as deaneries, parishes, diocesan departments – to make plans that will describe their share in the delivery of the overall strategy. The team leading the implementation phase will need to provide guidance and offer both challenge and support. They should expect to see and comment on all the plans being made.

The objective here is not to command adherence to a diocesan directive – hardly possible anyway! – but to invite all the key players to develop their plans in the light of the framework they have helped to create. If the engagement phase has been managed well, people should already be thinking about what the new vision and strategy will require of them and should welcome the chance to capture and develop this thinking. A delicate balance is required – it may be wise to assure parishes they will not be coerced into making plans to suit the diocese. At the same time, leadership must be clear and consistent in the expectation that planning and implementation will take place across the diocese. Leadership can be more directive with diocesan departments but, in general, a kind of polite persistence is better than anything that feels like a heavy hand on the shoulder.

In a parish, the planning process need not be elaborate – it may well be a matter of asking key groups to make simple plans. If the strategy involves a major new activity such as a building project, then the process will necessarily be more demanding and is likely to require a new, dedicated group to undertake it.

What should a plan cover? This will be familiar territory for many, and some will be relieved to arrive at a more congenial stage in the process. Essentially the plan should list key objectives (what you want to do), activities (what you will do to achieve them), timescales (when things will happen), milestones (key stages in the achievement of the goals), outcomes (the difference that will be made), measurables (how you will know you have achieved the outcome) and responsibilities (who will make what happen) – and the budget required. If the right people are present the planning process could be initiated at the launch event, if held.

Finally, planning should not take too long, nor become over-elaborated as a way of avoiding action. As soon as possible, plans should be enacted.

Critical success factors

There are some factors and principles that are critical to the success of the implementation phase.

Behaviour is more important than process

One of Telos Partners' earliest assignments was to help a major insurance company set up a new direct retail arm. The client had started by spending millions of pounds setting up a new customer relations management process and accompanying software. They realized only later how little this would avail them unless the new business stood for something that its staff believed in and were able to express in the way they interacted with customers. We helped them develop a shared understanding of the values of the new business and the behaviour required to make those values live.

In general, changed behaviours are more significant and have greater impact than changed processes and structures – too many change initiatives start with the latter and peter out. The truth is that motivated people doing the right things will make flawed structures and processes work, but fine processes and structures will not make up for unhelpful behaviours and lack of motivation.

It may well be wise to reorganize the diocesan departments or change the number and size of deaneries, but that should be the final step in the process, not the starting point. Far more will be achieved if individuals act more positively, exercise more responsibility and accept the behavioural implications of whatever you have decided together you wish to achieve.

The strategy should be clear about how values will be translated into behaviour – this should remain the focus in the implementation phase.

Developing skills

Another significant factor will be the extent to which the parish, diocese or organization offers opportunities for people to develop their capabilities. If you are asking them to do new things they need an opportunity to acquire the necessary new awareness and skills. This could become a major activity because there may be many groups and individuals in a diocese who would benefit from development programmes designed to support the new strategy. Such programmes are also a marvellous opportunity to build collaboration, provide a forum for addressing problems, reinforce the desired culture and encourage positive attitudes and ways of behaving. If a large-scale bespoke programme is too big an ask, then at least the diocesan education and training departments should be developing their plans to ensure that all their regular training and learning programmes are, if necessary, completely re-thought and support the new strategy.

Leadership

The leadership team has a vital role. It must be united and consistent in its messages and continue to talk about and reinforce the new direction; it must model the new behaviours and demonstrate determination and persistence. This requires leaders, in a paraphrase of Gandhi's words, to 'be the change they want to see'. Without it there will be a – probably accurate – perception that there is one rule for 'them' and another for 'us'. The change process will stagnate because people do not see the kind of leadership that inspires confidence and builds the sense that we are all in this together. This means that the team should continue to give attention to its own performance and that of its members.

The team also needs to be a place where support for one another is real and expressed through honest feedback and acceptance of collective responsibility. This might sound straightforward and obvious but it may prove extremely challenging amid a change process. If the team cannot remain united and focused, there will be considerable confusion in the wider organization.

Persistence and evaluation

If change is to stick, persistence is required. Organizations need to take positive action to embed new ways of working. If this is lacking, people are likely to feel that their cynical impulses were justified – 'We knew it was all talk and we were right.'

Not everything works straightaway and not all ideas will prove effective in practice. Progress must be measured and action taken to address parts of the implementation that are not working out as planned. If this is not done, confidence in the whole process can be undermined by a small number of perhaps relatively minor failures.

Summary of actions

1 If required, create a change team.
2 Initiate and follow through a business planning process.
3 Provide any necessary learning and development support.
4 Maintain united and focused leadership.
5 Listen to those who are unhappy with change.
6 Stick with it; see it through.

10

Keep it fresh

After all this, what have you got? You should have a group of people who share an understanding of why you are here, what matters to you and what you are trying to achieve. They should be working together to realize the Church's vision, with a pretty clear idea of what they need to do to make their contribution. You are actively creating the future of the Church and addressing any particular problems that prompted you to enter this process. You have a clear idea of what you are trying to do, how you are going to do it, and you know what to measure to know whether you are being successful or not. You will not have entered the sunny uplands of effortless progress because the world is not like that. But you will know where you are going and why, and will be seeing the Church's ministry bearing a great deal more fruit. I think that is worth the effort and hope you will agree.

One of the main benefits will be that the process, if done well, will create a new sense of unity, hope and energy. People will have enjoyed it and feel a new sense of kinship with those with whom they have worked. There will be a sense of having been together on a rich, challenging and ultimately satisfying journey.

Renewal

The final stage in the process we have been using is renewal. In this stage we recognize that creating the future is not an activity one does once, it is a continuing challenge. The point of the Trialogue introduced in Chapter 2 is less to encourage a one-off development of strategy than the habit of continuous adaptation. What might that mean?

At a formal level it probably means building into the timetable opportunities for review and renewal of vision, strategy and plans. But that is only part of the story. If you have carried through the process suggested in this book you will have established a new way of thinking and working. This can be characterized as an organized conversation in which everyone has a part to play in the creation of the future. The conversation itself is characterized by a willingness to listen, understand, share insights and accept responsibility together for the cause we share. It is nowadays considered highly desirable to be a 'learning organization'. This does not refer to an organization that values formal learning opportunities so much as one that habitually shares insights, expertise and is willing to adapt and grow in response to those insights. In a learning organization there is an individual and corporate recognition that organizational and personal growth is a product of our common willingness to seek, share and respond to new experiences and information – above all to respond to changes in the environment; that is, in the world in which we operate.

So the challenge at this stage in the process is to find mechanisms for keeping the conversation going. In a parish it may be relatively easy to 'hard wire' this in the use of sermons, cell groups, PCC, parish newsletter and so forth. It will be harder for the diocese – but it will probably involve a more joined-up and deliberate use of senior staff visits and preaching opportunities, use of new digital media as well as traditional communication tools and creative use of the agendas set for synods.

Above all though, keeping the conversation going is about a shared concern and habit of mind, and it will be maintained as much in informal as formal settings. All this will mean a level of openness and engagement with one another and a greater sharing of responsibility than we are generally used to. It ought to have the effect of continuing to strengthen relationships, even where there remain profound differences of opinion.

Succession

In other organizations the renewal phase will also involve succession planning, which recognizes that good work can be continued and built upon – or undermined – when leadership changes. This is not a straightforward subject in the Church, where structures and processes may not help. A number of external bodies are involved in appointments, such as patrons and, to some degree at the most senior level, government. There can be a lack of joined-up thinking and process – though there are many who work hard to mitigate these difficulties. Bishops are usually able to influence parish appointments, but this will only help if they understand and support what parishes have been doing. Clearly this would be more likely if the development of strategy has involved the whole diocese as well as individual parishes.

Fortunately, local congregations do have a veto in the choice of new clergy. They would be wise to do what they can to ensure the new leader builds upon what has been achieved rather than undoes it all, not just in terms of the content but, if possible, the style – if the new vicar likes to operate as a one-man band, the new culture may be damaged.

In dioceses it has often been the case that a bishop who has led positive change is succeeded by someone with a very different approach. This was often the result of a deliberate policy of balancing interests and styles over time. Thus a more evangelical bishop was likely to be followed by a more catholic one; a reformer by one likely to provide a different form of leadership – more pastoral or intellectual, for example. This would sometimes lead to an unhelpful change of direction or stagnation in the change process. My understanding is that though something of this impulse for balance remains, the approach has changed – there is certainly more awareness of the needs of the diocese in the national appointments process. Nevertheless, senior staff and elected representatives in dioceses should do what they can to encourage the appointment of someone who will continue the good work.

The national Church

As far as the Church of England as a whole is concerned, the time has come to stop reacting and start acting. The institution is always lagging behind events despite its myriad examples of good practice and faithful service and its still vital role in the lives of many communities and individuals. The Church needs to consider and articulate its identity and role in contemporary terms; it needs to describe a better vision for its future and its strategy for getting there; it needs to engage all its members in these deliberations and decisions – and then take action. The process described in this book would require considerable adaptation for a national engagement with the future of the Church, but the basic principles would not change. What an exciting and engaging process it could be! Where I have seen it undertaken by Christian organizations (albeit on a smaller scale), those involved have found it compelling, energizing and spiritually renewing. The opportunity is there to be grasped and only awaits a leadership that sees the value and is willing to make the commitment.

Notes

Introduction

1 For example, Peter Rudge, *Management in the Church* (London: McGraw-Hill, 1976).

1 Face the facts

1 To be precise, parishes raised £896.6m in 2010. Total Church of England income was £1.299bn. Financial overview provided by the Financial Policy Unit of the Archbishops' Council, available on Church of England website.

2 Christian Research – <www.christian-research.org>.

3 Church Statistics 2010, available on Church of England website.

4 Christian Research.

5 Monica Furlong, *The C of E: The State It's In* (London: Hodder & Stoughton, 2000).

6 Mike Clinton, Experiences of Ministry Survey 2011, Respondents Findings Report, Church of England and King's College London.

7 Average weekly attendance – Church of England statistics department and reported on Church of England website.

8 There is a full discussion of the causes and lessons of contemporary church growth in Bob Jackson, *Hope for the Church: Contemporary Strategies for Growth* (London: Church House, 2002) and his other books.

2 Get organized

1 See especially P. Dudley, 'Quality Management or Management Quality?', PhD dissertation, University of Hull, 2000.

2 Sponsored by the Royal Society of Arts, Manufactures and Commerce (RSA) 1993; final report published 1995.

3 Jim Collins and Jerry I. Porras, *Built to Last: Successful Habits of Visionary Companies* (London: Random House, 1994).

4 Jim Collins, *Good to Great: Why Some Companies Make the Leap . . . and Others Don't* (London: Random House, 2001).

5 Michael E. Porter, *Competitive Strategy: Techniques for Analyzing Industries and Competitors* (New York: Free Press, 1980).

6 See Richard Beckhard, *Organization Development: Strategies and Models*, (Reading, MA: Addison-Wesley, 1969). The formula has a tangled history. It appears Gleicher and Beckhard developed it but Beckhard and Harris

published it – Richard Beckhard and Reuben Harris *Organizational Transitions: Managing Complex Change* (Reading, MA: Addison-Wesley, 1987). It was given its current expression by Kathleen Dannemiller – see Kathleen D. Dannemiller and Robert W. Jacobs, 'Changing the Way Organizations Change: A Revolution of Common Sense', *Journal of Applied Behavioral Science*, 28(4), 1992, pp. 480–98.

3 Trust the process

1 Experiences of Ministry Survey 2011 Respondent Findings Report, p. 6.
2 Regional Training Partnerships were recommended in the report of a working party set up by the Archbishops' Council. The 2003 report was entitled 'Formation for Ministry within a Learning Church: The Structure and Funding of Ordination Training' but is more usually described as the Hind Report, after the working party's chairman, Bishop John Hind. It considered ways of rationalizing training provision and recommended the establishment of ecumenical RTPs to develop more effective regional training strategies – ensuring that resources are used well, duplication avoided and gaps filled.

4 Get on the 'T'

1 Bernard M. Bass and Ronald E. Riggio, *Transformational Leadership*, 2nd edn (London: Taylor & Francis, 2005); Robert K. Greenleaf, *Servant Leadership: A Journey into the Nature of Legitimate Power and Greatness* (Mahwah, NJ: Paulist Press, 2002); John Adair, *Inspiring Leadership: Learning from Great Leaders* (London: Thorogood 2002); Richard E. Boyatzis and Annie McKee, *Resonant Leadership: Renewing Yourself and Connecting with Others through Mindfulness, Hope, and Compassion* (Boston: Harvard Business School Press, 2005); Marcy L. Shankman and Scott J. Allen, *Emotionally Intelligent Leadership: A Guide for College Students* (San Francisco, CA: Jossey-Bass, 2008); Bill George, *Authentic Leadership: Rediscovering the Secrets to Creating Lasting Value* (San Francisco, CA: Jossey-Bass, 2004).
2 See for example, Greenleaf, *Servant Leadership*.
3 When I use terms like 'senior' I am talking about the role occupied by the individual rather than about his or her status. The suggestion that people 'at the top' of organizations focus on future and identity issues is made because they are in a position in the organization that allows them to see the whole better than anyone else. They are, and should remain, 'on the balcony'. This is a vital organizational function but does not make them more important or better than anyone else. People in organizational leadership roles are of necessity a little distanced from the day-to-day operation and so should refrain from interfering in it.

4 *Building a Picture of Episcope: An Agenda for Action and Characteristics of Episcope.*

5 This would be right and reasonable – though there is another perspective. Some of the leaders who have the greatest impact are strikingly *unrea-sonable* – refuse to conform to commonly accepted expectations, demand an exceptional level of performance from themselves and others, sacrifice a great deal to achieve the goal and refuse to be daunted by any obstacle. We have had plenty of these in the Church, from St Paul to Mother Teresa.

5 Create a team

1 Jon R. Katzenbach and Douglas K. Smith, *The Wisdom of Teams: Creating the High-Performance Organization* (Boston: Harvard Business School Press, 1993).

2 See Richard Beckhard, *Organization Development: Strategies and Models*, (Reading, MA: Addison-Wesley, 1969) and Kathleen D. Dannemiller and Robert W. Jacobs, 'Changing the Way Organizations Change: A Revolution of Common Sense', *Journal of Applied Behavioral Science*, 28(4), 1992, pp. 480–98.

3 Bruce W. Tuckman, 'Developmental Sequence in Small Groups', *Psychological Bulletin* 63(6), 1965, pp. 384–99.

6 Know who you are

1 See for example Jim Collins and Jerry I. Porras, *Built to Last: Successful Habits of Visionary Companies* (London: Random House, 1994), and the report, published in 1995, of the 'Tomorrow's Company Inquiry', spon-sored by the Royal Society of Arts, Manufactures and Commerce.

2 See <www.newscorp.com/corp_gov/sobc_conclusion.html>.

3 Some deny it is an organization. It has been described to me as more like a coalition or an organism. These descriptions have validity and relevance but do not contradict seeing the Church as an organization. The Church of England has common disciplines, a consistency of structure, a set of shared practices, a single decision-making body, boundaries and an organizational hierarchy. When people say it is not an organization, do they mean it is not an organization in the bureaucratic machine mould associated with large corporations (in the imagination of some, if not in fact)? But organizations appear in many forms and guises and many of these are described precisely as organisms or political alliances. There is a good discussion of the metaphors we use to understand organiza-tions in Gareth Morgan, *Images of Organization*, updated edn (London: Sage, 2006). The Church of England is an unusual organization, but

an organization nevertheless. The issue is how it can best be effective in representing Christ to the English people.

4 Jan Cooney and Kevin Burton, *Photolanguage Australia Human Values (A and B)* (Sydney: Catholic Education Office, 1986).

7 Decide where you want to go

1 Robert Burns, 'To a Mouse'.
2 Hebrews 12.2.
3 Office of National Statistics projection – <www.statistics.gov.uk>.
4 Jim Collins, *Good to Great: Why Some Companies Make the Leap . . . and Others Don't* (London: Random House, 2001).

9 Make it happen

1 Referred to in Robert Hockley's unpublished seminar notes.

Further reading

A short list of some of the books I have found helpful.

Beckford, John, *Quality: A Critical Introduction*, 3rd edn (London: Routledge, 2009).

Beer, Stafford, *Diagnosing the System: For Organizations* (Chichester: Wiley, 1985).

Collins, Jim, *Good to Great: Why Some Companies Make the Leap . . . and Others Don't* (London: Random House, 2001).

Collins, Jim and Jerry I. Porras, *Built to Last: Successful Habits of Visionary Companies* (London: Random House, 1994).

Handy, Charles, *The Hungry Spirit: Beyond Capitalism – A Quest for Purpose in the Modern World* (London: Hutchinson, 1997).

Jackson, Bob, *Hope for the Church: Contemporary Strategies for Growth* (London: Church House Publishing, 2002).

Kübler-Ross, Elisabeth, *On Death and Dying* (London: Routledge, 1969).

Lamdin, Keith, *Finding Your Leadership Style: A Guide for Ministers* (London: SPCK, 2012) – a helpful summary of the various approaches to leadership and a good guide to implementation for ministers.

Levi, Daniel, *Group Dynamics for Teams*, 3rd edn (London: Sage, 2011).

Morgan, Gareth, *Images of Organization*, updated edn (London: Sage, 2006).

Percy, Martyn and Ian Markham (eds), *Why Liberal Churches are Growing* (London: T & T Clark, 2006).

Porter, Michael E., *Competitive Strategy: Techniques for Analyzing Industries and Competitors* (New York: Free Press, 1980).

Rosenzweig, Phil, *The Halo Effect . . . and the Eight other Business Delusions that Deceive Managers* (London: Free Press, 2007) – an excellent and enjoyable critique of Collins and others.

Wilson, Steve, *Reflections and Challenges* (London: Telos Partners, 2010) – a product of interviews carried out with a range of clients about sustainable success; available free from Telos Partners – see www.telospartners.com.